Happy Ch
Basings

A Jolly Christmas,
and may
Good Luck
"PURSUE" you in the New Year.
From F. Smythe to Philip.

Compiled by

BASINGSTOKE
TALKING HISTORY

Edited by
Barbara Applin

Published by the Basingstoke Archaeological & Historical Society
First published 2009

ISBN 978-0-9508095-5-7

Printed and bound by YesPrint www.yesprint.co.uk

**A Huge Thank You to the Hampshire
& Isle of Wight Community Foundation
whose Grassroots grant made this
publication possible.**

Acknowledgements
BASINGSTOKE TALKING HISTORY are most grateful to the *Basingstoke Gazette*
for permission to publish extracts from *Arthur Attwood's Look into the Past* and issues
of the *Gazette* and to *Hampshire, the County Magazine* for extracts from *Christmas in
Basingstoke* by John Arlott (December 1966).
For photographs we thank the Hampshire County Museum Service (title page, pp 25,
29 The Rev. Chute, 53, 60, 63, 73, 76, 80 top, 86 and colour pp 1, 2); the *Gazette* (pp
40, 41, 43, 48, 49, 82, 91, 92); www.basingstokevideofilmmakers.co.uk (pp 6, 95 and
colour p 4, bottom); David Mann (pp 94, 95 bottom, colour page 4, top two);   James
A M Phillips (p 4 top two); Festival Place (pp 4 bottom, 38); Robert Brown (pp 19,
27, 28, 68); Royal Mail Group; (p68); Jo Kelly (pp 80, 81; Bob Applin (p 72) and The
Turton Collection (p 97 dance card); Debz Charlton, page 98. And people interviewed
for photos, cards and posters they allowed us to scan. It was not always possible to
locate copyright holders and we hope any we have overlooked will forgive us.
Cover illustration & colour page 3 Anita Leatherby; cover design Ann Paganuzzi.

References
A History of the Ancient Town & Manor of Basingstoke, F J Baigent & J E
Millward (Basingstoke & London, 1889); *A History of the Vyne in Hampshire*
Chaloner W Chute (London 1888); *The Mays of Basingstoke*, R Ray (London &
Basingstoke 1904); *Jane Austen: A Life*, Claire Tomalin (Viking 1997); *Within
Living Memory* Diana Stanley (Basingstoke 1968); *Victoria County History* Volume
4, p140); *1895: A Year in the Life of Ethel Lizzie Moody*. ed Brian Butler (Cardiff
2003)

Preface

A hundred years ago, Cecil Sharp and his circle began collecting English traditional folk songs, rescuing many from oblivion. More recently, many veterans of the Second World War, who had long locked up and deeply buried their personal recollections of those momentous times, have started to share their experiences with families and friends. Today, more and more people live life in the fast lane as high speed internet communications and social networks transform the way we live. Are these seemingly unrelated features of modern history linked in any way? If so, how?

'Happy Christmas, Basingstoke!' is a collection of memories of how the people of Basingstoke passed this Special Time in the recent and not so recent past. To my mind it is part of the wonderful tradition that Cecil Sharp illustrated so clearly that we all have a responsibility to recall and record what goes on around us. A responsibility certainly, but also a pleasure that contributes directly to our very own cultural heritage and helps to define that very elusive quality of what it means to be British.

At a time when new arrivals to our country from other parts of the global village have to pass a 'Britishness test' to stay amongst us, I believe we all should examine what it means to us as individuals to be part of our own society. With more and more of us exploring and discovering our own family histories, documents like *'Happy Christmas, Basingstoke!'* have an important part to play in defining just what made us tick in the past, and can provide an observation platform from which to compare how we all live today.

The Basingstoke Archaeological & Historical Society is to be complimented on this latest publication in the Basingstoke Talking History series. I warmly commend it to anyone who has an interest in the past, their families, the town and borough in which we live, and the times through which we are passing. It's a good read, and should be a must for your stocking fillers this coming Christmas.

Brian Gurden
Mayor
9 August 2009

Decorations at the Gazette office.

At the top of town.

And at Festival Place.

4

Introduction

One day in 1994, Mary Felgate, then 82, picked up a cassette recorder and spoke into it her memories of Christmas as a child in Basingstoke. She even sang the song she used to sing with her father when they washed up after Christmas tea! This was the inspiration for the Basingstoke Talking History group of the Basingstoke Archaeological & Historical Society to search the interviews they and the Museum had recorded (over 290 in the collection now) for other Christmas memories. We went on to interview many others who, between them, have given such a vivid and varied picture, not just of the Christmas period itself but of the preparations that sometimes had begun months before.

Collecting, transcribing and editing these memories has been a fascinating job, calling for real team work. Some of the memories we have captured are of experiences that many people will have shared, some are very detailed and clear, some are poignant and some are simply surprising.

We have interspersed the extracts from recorded interviews with extracts from books and articles in magazines and newspapers, and we are grateful to the copyright holders for permission to include them. The Hampshire Museums & Archives Service have been particularly helpful in providing photographs, as have the organisers of the Hospital Pantomime, and many individuals allowed us to use others, precious pieces of family archives. The black and white line drawings are by our own members: Anita Leatherby, Alan and Nicola Turton and Jane Baker (Magi). Editorial comments are in italics like this; extracts from books on a 'turned-back page' as below, and other printed material is in boxes.

Thinking of the long Christmas to New Year holiday that many people have today, it was **Arthur Attwood** in 1980 who pointed out how very different things once were.

Barbara Applin

Fifty years ago, they would have to be content with Christmas Day and Boxing Day, with work continuing up to 5 pm or later on Christmas Eve.

The Build-up to Christmas

Preparing for the panto

'Christmas starts earlier every year!' Well, some preparations really do start very early. The Basingstoke Hospital Pantomime is a regular part of Christmas and the New Year, but **John Ramage** *and* **Julie Jones** *explain how it has evolved over many years and just how much time and hard work goes into it. In their 'day jobs' John is Consultant in Gastroenterology and Julie is a Clinical Audit Facilitator at The Ark.*

Although the pantomime is in January, script writing starts as early as April/May in preparation for auditions in September. At auditions a rehearsal schedule is given out so that people who want to be involved can see what their commitment would be and they can then sort out their shifts if required. We have rehearsals once a week after work hours, and also some at weekends. We're not professional, it's all voluntary and it is very difficult to get all the cast together, but we do manage it in the end. We always have consultants in the panto every year - I'm sure they're the crowd-puller! Because they're very busy we write the script so that they're only in one or two scenes and don't have to come to all the rehearsals. But we do try to get them to come to at least one so they can see where they fit in, and also to the technical and dress rehearsals at the end.

Consultants:
Dr Carl Brookes
Dr Simon Keightley
Dr Andrew Bishop

6

John Pritchard, an administrator, wrote quite a lot of scripts over about five or six years. It was a lot of work for one person to do, and for the last few years a script writers group has been formed, made up of several of the panto actors, so now the task is a collaborative effort. We get an outline of the story and work out how we're going to make it into an NHS hospital-type panto, like 'The Sound of Mucus'. Of course, when you start acting, it all changes again! This year the Basingstoke Amateur Theatrical Society's Young Generation Group are allowing us to rehash their Dick Whittington script. We have already changed the name to 'Sick Whittington' to mirror recent pantos we have done.

Paul Robinson puts all the sound effects on a CD, and we have two great choreographers here (Tammie Purdue and Tamasin Beckett) who work out the dance routines. We started off just making up the music by ear from a very simple score, but then a few people turned up to arrange the music for several instruments and that grew until we had about twelve or fifteen people playing in a band called 'Surgical Spirit'. We've simplified the music now, with lots of songs and dances played on CD; however, there is nothing like 'live' music and we are very fortunate to have Debbie Lewis, the keyboard player and Simon Baggaley, a drummer, and sometimes also a guitar player.

It's amazing how much time people are prepared to put into it all, with the preparations right through the year.

Giant	*Fe Fi Fo Fum* *I need food to fill my tum* *Bring me boys and girls to devour* *I want to eat one every hour.* *Hormonia, my serving maid, where are you?*
Hormonia	*The giant is an obstetrician and gynaecologist.*
Placenta Previa	*He has a hand in all sorts of things.*

Panto posters by Dr Jo Foley

Food for Christmas

As far back as the thirteenth century Basingstoke had to start preparing for Christmas at least a month beforehand. In their book **A History of the Ancient Manor and Town of Basingstoke,** *F W* **Baigent** *and* **J E Millard** *quoted the following order which had been sent out at the end of November 1250. Winchester was the capital then so the bailiffs who ran Basingstoke probably guessed that the Court would spend Christmas there as not much travelling was done in the winter months when the roads were so bad. If they had their wits about them, might they have anticipated the royal command and started fattening some hogs much earlier?*

King Henry III, having resolved to spend the festival of Christmas in his royal castle at Winchester, orders were sent to various neighbouring towns to furnish provisions for the occasion. On the 30th November a mandate was sent to the bailiffs of Basingstoke, commanding them to provide for the King's use two brawn hogs to be sent to Winchester against the feast of the Nativity.

Terry Tarrant, *until recently manager of the Maydown Farm Shop, said that even today the Christmas trade starts early.*

Christmas is interesting in the way that it's just changed so much over the years. It has become a big deal, probably the last part of our traditional life-style that maintains its importance in bringing families together. People do put themselves under a lot of pressure and have to plan so far ahead. And, with refrigeration and freezing, people can start thinking about Christmas and what they want to do. We have people placing orders for Christmas in October.

Even in ordinary families there is a lot to do before Christmas. People have to think ahead. **John Arlott**, *the famous BBC cricket commentator, was born in Basingstoke in 1914 and often wrote affectionately about the town. In an article first published in* **Hampshire: The County Magazine** *he tells how, when he was a boy in 1921, Christmas began really early.*

Mincemeat was made in October: currants were washed, raisins (seedless raisins lay still in the future) were stoned (and surreptitiously eaten) and candied peel - the huge rinds, red, yellow and green, with the wells of white melted sugar deep in the centre - chopped and chewed. Then, after the mincemeat, the Christmas pudding, made in time to 'improve' before Christmas and to allow for a 'taster' at the first Sunday dinner of December. Perhaps, too, there were paper chains to make; but most of ours were 'shop' ones - so elaborate that I fancy they were pre-1914 war - taken down every Twelfth Night, folded like concertinas and put away until the next Christmas. Certainly the main ones must have lasted us twenty years.

Judy Melluish has this plum pudding recipe which her aunt, Evelyn Bailey, had in the late 1930s from Cecily Kettle, the cook for Archdeacon Chute at the Rectory (which is now Chute House).

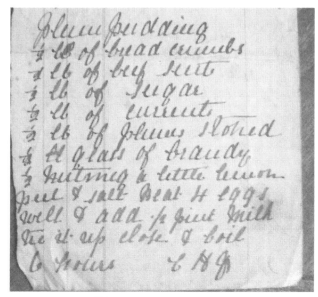

10

Christmas Clubs

*Children saved their pocket money to buy presents, while grown-ups saved through clubs run by shops, churches and pubs, such as the Slate Club and the Thrift Club, described by **Arthur Attwood** in his book* **Basingstoke: Arthur Attwood's Look into the Past.**

One of the biggest clubs met at the Church Street Methodist Schoolroom attached to the Wesleyan Methodist Church. This had a membership of several hundred. Most public-houses had their own club, the idea being that your weekly contributions enabled you to draw sick pay with the balance being shared between members at Christmas. Occasionally one would hear of a share-out not taking place in one of the pubs because someone had embezzled the funds.

__Hilda Applin__, who lived all her life in Basingstoke, is sitting second from the left in this 1930s photo of assistants at the International Stores in the Market Place. She describes her work before Christmas.

They used to run a Christmas Club and six weeks before Christmas you had to what they called 'work in' and we never got home much before ten o'clock. We had to weigh up so much stuff each night and everything had to be pre-packed. But, funny enough, I used to enjoy that time. Being young, we used to have sing-songs, we were allowed to sing while we were working, when the customers weren't there. We sang popular ones. 'What'll I do?' That was the one they used to sing quite a lot, 'What'll I do when you are far away, And I am blue. What'll I do?' Of course that tickled me, 'What'll I do?' And we had carols too.

They used to pay the club out about a fortnight before Christmas and we sometimes didn't get home till half past twelve at night. I remember going up Reading Road past the Salvation Army when the lights went out. There were no lights then after twelve o'clock. And I took to my heels and I don't think I stopped until I got to Coronation Road!

People wouldn't work like that now. You never had a penny overtime. And you didn't even get so much as a Happy Christmas!

Owen Blissett *was a child in the 1930s. His mother and aunts found the Christmas Clubs very useful.*

Before Christmas really arrived there was a big day out for all of the sisters, in that they all belonged to the International Stores' Christmas Club, and it was a ritual to go along and spend the money that they had invested in the club over the year and buy all the dried fruit, almonds, candied peel, icing sugar etc needed to make their Christmas cakes and puddings (nothing ready-made bought in those days, long before the days of pre-packed goods, everything had to be weighed up).

Park Prewett prepares

Dilys Eaton *tells of the pre-Christmas preparations she saw going on at Basingstoke's Park Prewett psychiatric hospital in 1954 when she became the librarian.*

At Park Prewett Hospital we took Christmas seriously; none of your twelve days, more like four weeks. At the beginning of December the Kitchen and the Supplies had their preparations well in hand; what they had to supply was no light matter: the traditional Christmas dinner for the twenty-odd inside wards, ten villas, Rooksdown House and Pinewood House was only part of it.

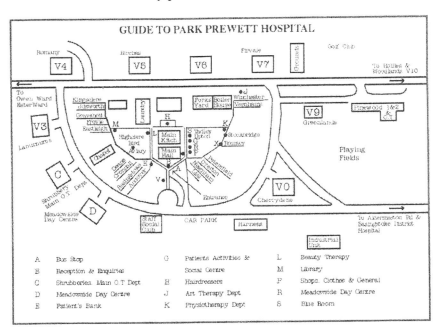

Traditionally the Works Department and the upholsterers decorated the Main Hall; they chose a theme each year and they produced some spectacular effects with no little danger to life and limb. On one occasion the upholsterer rigging up Father Christmas driving his sledge across the high, vaulted ceiling fell from the scaffolding, doing his legs considerably injury - fortunately he recovered.

From the beginning of the month there were gangs of patients and staff making paper roses, in aid of the Best Decorated Ward Competition - a cup was awarded each year. To my mind the best effect ever achieved was with a grove of real fir trees stretching down both sides of a long ward like an avenue - the whole place smelt deliciously of resin.

Advertisements

Advertisements in the **Hants & Berks Gazette** *show how the town's shopkeepers did their best to entice customers in the last few weeks and days before Christmas in the 1880s.*

A H Gaydon at The Fancy Repository in London Street:

Christmas and New Year cards at a discount.

F Blunden, also in London Street:

For the Christmas Season only: Half-guinea hamper: 1 bottle each of pale brandy, Irish whiskey, cordial gin, port and sherry. No. 1 Guinea Case: one bottle each of Martell's brandy, best Irish whiskey, best Scotch whiskey and good sound port, and two bottles each of best gin and good pale sherry. No. 2 Guinea Case: 1 bottle each of champagne and sparkling hock, 2 bottles each of port and marsala and three bottles of sherry.

Benjamin Owen Johnson in the Market Place was gentlemen's outfitter, general draper and silk mercer, dressmaker, milliner and undertaker.

For Christmas Presents & New Year Gifts: Ladies' Cashmere Circular Cloaks, Black Fur Capes & Muffs and Ladies' Knitted Wool Petticoats; as well as Novelties in Fancy Boxes.

Terry Tarrant, until recently at the Manydown Farm Shop, was always particularly busy just before Christmas.

My Christmas trade would probably be something in the region of three and a half to four weeks' worth of trade in a week. Certainly the turkey side of the business probably would be something like 500 to 600 turkeys. Christmas is a large part of our trading. The years of selling whole turkeys and not preparing them for the oven has changed a lot. There are now more turkeys being boned out, stuffed or rolled, or even parts of turkeys being sold now than ever before. I think meatwise we are still selling certainly as much as we were twenty or thirty years ago for Christmas - it's very much a two- or three-joint product time of year; most people seem to want a turkey and a ham and a joint of beef or a joint of lamb - and tongues, last year (2008) we sold more tongues than we sold in any other year and we only seem to sell them at Christmas.

The **Hants & Berks Gazette** *for 22nd December 1883 reported that many shop windows were decorated for Christmas.*

WINDOW DRESSING

Some of the grocers and other tradesmen of the town have made their shops gay with the emblems of the season, and among these Mr. Sapp, Mr. Owen, Mr. Wadmore, Mr. Glanville, Mr. Cane, and the London and County Tea Company have been very successful. A novelty, in the shape of a bicycle race, in the window of Mr. J. H. Baker's establishment, attracted large crowds of spectators, and created considerable excitement.

The trade directories of the time give more information about the shopkeepers mentioned in this advertisement:

Meatyard & Sapp, Chemists and Grocers.

J Owen, Restaurant, Cook, Confectioner, Dealer in English & foreign fruits etc, High Street, Basingstoke.

Walter Wadmore, Wholesale & Retail Grocer, Winchester Road, Mayor 1890-1, 1902-3, then living at Brook House, Brook Street.

Glanville, Tea dealers, Grocers, Bakers and Provision Merchants.

Joseph Cane, Grocery & Provision Stores, Station Hill.

J H Baker, Grocer, Tea Dealer and Provision Merchant, Church Street, had raisins, currants and prunes as specialities for Christmas, figs, oranges, nuts etc, Huntley & Palmer's fancy biscuits and cakes, good family tea, Prime Home-cured Wiltshire, Hambro' and Canadian bacon and Home-cured Irish and Canadian hams. As a further inducement, he announced, 'Goods delivered in the country and carriage paid on all parcels.'

It started at Christmas

Why hold a cattle sale at Christmas? It was obviously a success, as was mentioned in an article by **Arthur Saunders**. *He was a reporter for the* **Hants & Berks Gazette** *from 1928 and its editor from 1948 to 1960.*

> The Basingstoke Market, near the Station was founded by Mr. Hugh E Raynbird, a practical farmer and one of the leading experts on agricultural matters in his day. The first Christmas cattle sale was held in 1873. Its success suggested the holding of monthly sales. The suggestion was adopted and it was not long before the monthly sales became fortnightly ones, and these in turn weekly sales.

More decorations & displays

As a child, in about 1917-20, **Mary Felgate** *loved seeing how the shops were decorated.*

When it got near Christmas it was a great thing to be taken out in the evening and go round and look at all the decorations. The shops used to really go to town, making wonderful displays for Christmas. And even in the evening all the lights were on over the shops because people were living there, there were always people coming in and out.

At Christmas times Lanham's stores was always decorated with wonderful Chinese lanterns hanging everywhere. Those lanterns expressed Christmas to me, as we always had one or two at home, hung well away from the gas lights, but in later days with electricity they could be hung over the electric light bulbs. Although Aunt Lizzie in the Church Street bookshop did sell small Christmas paper chains and packets of paper for making up the chains, and Christmas toys and cards and calendars, I never remember seeing any decorations whatsoever in her house. I suppose, being a Brethren family, they were too strict for such worldly things. But Aunt Lizzie always enjoyed the Christmas trade.

*Writing in 1966, **John Arlott** remembered how, as a boy in 1921, he had enjoyed window-shopping.*

Turn left along Winchester Street. Street lighting had not then reached the present uniformity which sheds a cool even clarity everywhere. At some points the gaslights were massed so that they flowered in a huge yellow glory. Nothing in any modern shopping centre stands out, or conveys such an outstanding impression of splendour as Lanham's windows used to do at Christmas in Basingstoke, forty-odd years ago. There was any amount of cotton -wool snow, sprinkled with glittering white metal filings and dotted with tiny figures of Father Christmas. There was a *real* Father Christmas inside but we knew him puncturingly as 'only old Fred from along May Street' - and expensive at that.

The main attraction in that year of post-war revelation was a clockwork train, running round its rails, over points, past a signal and through a station. As it disappeared beyond the window on every fourth circuit, its return was delayed while some bored, underpaid assistant wound it up; but we were not impatient. No real train was ever awaited by its passengers with more affection than that jerky, dark-green engine with its four wobbly carriages and guard's van.

At the last of the toy windows - to be saved until the end and eyed with something near reverence, far beyond hope - appeared a bicycle - not just an ordinary bicycle but a *boy's* bicycle - small, all shining and black, and with a pump and saddle-bag - 'The Bike'. We knew every angle and item of it; the line of the handlebars, the shape of the saddle; we used to stare at it, speechless.

Shops then were more colourful. Less hygienic, perhaps, but they showed their goods - often sprawling far across the pavement - in vast profusion.

The butchers hung their shop fronts with poultry carcases and evergreens, and they crammed all their windows with pies, ox-tongues, bladders of lard, pigs' heads with lemons in their mouths and mighty joints so prodigally that it was a wonder their assistants found time to display them all and put them away in the same day.

Wilkinson, at the fruit and flower shop in New Street, was reckoned the finest window-dresser in the town (it is intriguing to wonder where he might have gone and done in these days) and his windows were always exciting, but especially at Christmas time. He could arrange fruit - particularly the most highly polished apples I have ever seen - with flowers - and vegetables, like celery, which he could make *look* like a flower - in such patterns that his window was a picture to arrest even the eyes of toy-obsessed schoolboys.

The market went on late on Saturdays and Wednesdays before Christmas, the naphtha lamps hissed and whipped their smoke-capped flames in lurid shapes across the winter night and 'The Orange King', 'The China King', 'The Chocolate King' and 'The Potato King' hollered themselves hoarse.

Their goods, spilled by high-speed hurling into bags,
rolled and shivered across the ground.

Arthur Attwood's account of Christmas preparations in 1928 might surprise children today. Do children still help to stir the pudding?

Many people did not go to the butchers for their Christmas lunch, for they often killed their own chicken and pigs. Back-garden fowl were commonplace, so, too, were pigs on the allotments. A familiar sound during the run-up to Christmas would be the squealing of pigs when slaughtering was taking place on the allotments, such as May Street, where the Dry family were among the pig keepers.

In those days children did not only help Mother stir the pudding, but lent a hand in plucking the cockerel or chicken while it was still warm. Another task we loved doing was helping with the decorations by making paper-chains. We would go either to Bartlett's in Wote Street or Whiteman's in Church Street to buy a pot of gum and strips of coloured paper.

But there were other preparations for Christmas: one had to make sure that there was enough coal in the shed. Those who could afford a half-ton would count the sacks being carried from the horse-drawn coal-cart which bore the sign '2/7d a hundredweight'. The suppliers would be Stephens & Phillips, Ballards, the Basingstoke Co-operative Society, Hopgoods, Toomers etc.

Just before Christmas the wise would have their chimneys swept - and what an upset it would be when the begrimed Mr Bull, Mr Banyard or Mr Hutchings arrived, usually before breakfast.

Children who were up would watch for the brush to come out through the chimneypot.

Another essential was paraffin and one man who tried to keep faith with his customers was 'Punch' Avery who lived in a cottage at the Victory Square, Brook Street.

Long into the evening one could see a faint light on a barrow approaching: it would be bowler-hatted 'Punch' completing his rounds, which covered the whole of Basingstoke. He was a real character and a contemporary of 'Happy Bob', another who traded from a truck, but in his case it was fruit and winkles. His permanent pitch was outside the Barge yard at the bottom of Wote Street.

Late shopping on a market day just before Christmas could be quite exciting with the kerosene flares lighting up the stalls - and, of course, the thrill of meeting Father Christmas.

He was always in attendance at Lanham's, whose toy shop in those days was on the south side of Winchester Street. There was also the bran-tub where we kids could have a dig for three-pence, sixpence or a shilling and for those prices there could be something well worth having.

Betty Blake's family came to Basingstoke in 1936 and she has lived here ever since.

There was a thriving market on Wednesday and Saturday outside the former Town Hall, now the Willis Museum. Stalls, set round the sides of the Market Square, were largely owned by traders from town shops, family businesses.

One of the stallholders was a Mr Paine who owned a greengrocer's shop near the Wote Street end of the Lesser Market. On Saturday evenings he sold everything at reduced prices. I well recall that bananas were sold at 6d per dozen - this, of course, was prior to the 1939-45 War and the introduction of Ration Books.

At Christmas time many of the stallholders sold holly and mistletoe which looked very attractive in the sputtering light from the acetylene lamps (which would certainly not conform to modern Health and Safety Regulations).

Graham Kirby *remembers Christmas in the 1930s.*

When I was about ten or eleven, we'd go up to the old Market Square, probably eight o'clock on a Saturday night, and it was quite nice to be up there of an evening, in the dark, with all the stalls lit with the old lamps and the Salvation Army band playing. They used to play outside the International Stores at the top of the Market Square. And all that sort of thing didn't cost any money but we just used to enjoy it.

Betty Godden *had problems with wartime shortages. The shop she mentions is the one in Church Street that had been run by Mary Felgate's aunt about forty years earlier. What a contrast with Mary's account (page 17)!*

Returning to the area in the Second World War, it was impossible at Christmas to buy coloured wrapping paper, but one small shop, by St Michael's, in Church Street, had a few Christmas sticky labels to add to the plain brown paper in which to wrap presents one had made for family and friends.

Audrey Peryer's *family were newcomers to Basingstoke in 1958.*

Well, we didn't have a lot, I can tell you! And my parents came to see us over the Christmas period, but getting ready for Christmas was a bit hair-raising because we went down into Basingstoke to do the shopping and the crowds everywhere were unbelievable, you know! Everybody fighting to get their shopping in because there weren't many shops! We'd presumably managed to buy presents, various things. But there just wasn't any sort of variety of foods. There was only David Greig. Well, it wasn't even a supermarket, you had to queue up at each counter and get different bits. Oh, it seemed to take forever. And the market where you got all your vegetables. That's all there was of it, as far as I can remember.

Deborah Woodland *describes the food hall at the Co-op and the grotto for Father Christmas.*

I remember all sorts of different things being brought in there for Christmas. Boxes of biscuits absolutely stacked high, and all different colours. And you could always buy Christmas crackers in there. My mother used to collect the Co-op tokens. I'm sure she would spend them for different things at Christmas-time.

The Co-op was an important place at Christmas when you were five (1966)! I remember going to see Father Christmas in his grotto several years in a row. It was always upstairs next to the smaller flight of steps that led to the furniture department. It was just covered in Christmas wrapping paper, perfectly simple, nothing wrong with that. One year I chose a small cylindrical gift from a huge wicker basket in the grotto and was happy with the small doll I found inside. My sister chose a square package and wasn't pleased with the blue clip-together dolls' furniture it held – so we swapped! And that for me set up a bit of a life-long interest in dolls' houses, which my father used to make, and in the family we now have seven of them.

Deborah *also remembers the toys and bicycles at Gifford's and the windows at Thomas Wallis's.*

If you went upstairs in Gifford's, over the road, there were small toys but we had bicycles bought for us in Giffords and at Christmas that shop used to get so full I remember them suspending bicycles from 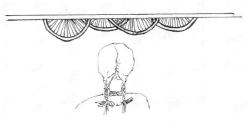 the ceiling, and I used to be fascinated, 'Well, how did they get them up there?'

Thomas Wallis's was a more old-fashioned shop, one of the older buildings, and I remember their window being decorated for Christmas, with writing in red, but I was too young to actually read it, presumably it said, 'Merry Christmas!' or something.

Generosity at Christmas

Christmas is traditionally seen as a time for giving. **The Victoria County History** *gives one instance from Basingstoke.*

William Blunden, who died in 1732, in his will devised £10 a year charged upon his lands and tenements in Surrey, to be distributed on Christmas Day amongst the poor.

From **The Hants & Berks Gazette.**

DECEMBER 22 1883

CHRISTMAS DINNER TO THE POOR

The subscriptions in behalf of this excellent object amounted to about £30.00. The applications for tickets took place on Thursday, when 220 were granted. It is proposed to distribute among these deserving persons no less than 800 pounds of meat. Mr. R. Knight has kindly discharged the duties of hon. treasurer, and Mr. J. A. Neville those of hon. sec.

JANUARY 12 1884

The School Children of the Basingstoke Union Workhouse were treated to their annual Christmas tree on Tuesday. There was an abundance of things to delight the youthful mind, provided through the kindness of the lady visitors, several of whom attended and did much to increase the happiness of the children.

In **The Mays of Basingstoke** *we hear how* **Colonel John May** *began his sixth Mayoralty of Basingstoke in 1901.*

Christmas was marked by great generosity on the part of the Mayor towards the poor of the town. His worship entrusted to a Committee the distribution of £50 worth of blankets and £25 worth of coal and wood amongst deserving families, gifts which were most highly appreciated.

He also made up a considerable balance on the Free Christmas Dinner Fund, thereby enabling the Committee to distribute a much larger quantity of meat than previously. Further, he doubled the amount of the Mayor's Christmas gifts to the inmates of the Almshouses in the town.

In an article in **The Hants & Berks Gazette** *in December 1880 the idea of Christmas goodwill was taken even further. This was a thinly disguised appeal on behalf of the SPCA (Society for the Prevention of Cruelty to Animals) who were campaigning against the ill-treatment of cab horses; it was probably syndicated in many newspapers.*

At the Christmas season when generous sentiments should certainly be in the ascendant, we trust a plea for the dumb servants of mankind, upon whom so many of our creature comforts depend, will not be regarded as out of place.

Jo Kelly *had some unhappy Sundays as a youngster in the '50s.*

I am a hoarder of books, I cannot part with any, I live surrounded by them. Now, I was a very lucky little girl, I had a Great Uncle Paul who was an illustrator for children's books and every Christmas a large box of books would arrive, a selection of books published that year by Collins and other publishing houses my Great Uncle had connections with. The box would contain one or possibly two girls' annuals.

There was always trouble in our house on the first Sunday in November each year. After lunch I would be handed a large box and be told to go through my books and select some for the Southern Railway Children's Orphanage at Woking. I would go upstairs, sit on my bed and start reading. Tea time would arrive and my Mother would come up to see how I had got on. Invariably it always ended in tears, as Mum would fill the box herself full of my precious books, telling me, as she did so, what an awful selfish girl I was. This I accepted but I used to offer to fill the box myself with my dresses and dolls, just leave me the books. It never worked. The next day my Father would take the box to work and it would travel up the line to Woking.

The Basingstoke Gazette *for 29th December 2008 reported on two Christmas events that were shining examples of the way people of all ages get together to entertain and to raise money for good causes at Christmas. At the Aldworth Science College more than 240 people enjoyed the annual Christmas Concert for elderly and disadvantaged residents organised by the Rotary Club of Basingstoke & Deane. The Hampshire County Youth Choir sang a range of traditional carols and 'other festive-themed numbers'.*

At The Anvil the Salvation Army organised A Christmas Gala *in aid of St Michael's Hospice. The Reading Central Timbrel Brigade was followed by the choir of Bishop Challoner School. The story of Jesus was read by Major Elaine Smith, with dancing and mime by young people from the Adventurers and the Jeannine Greville School of Dancing. Marc Harry of the Salvation Army sang popular songs which he had adapted or written himself. Then more songs by the Basingstoke Ladies' Choir and the Basingstoke Songster Brigade, music by the Salvation Army Band and a string quartet entitled* You'll know It. *And Major Ron Smith did tricks with a rope.*

Christmas Mail

Robert Brown, seen here, was a postman in the 1950s.

We had 14 walks in the whole of the town, because Basingstoke was much smaller in those days. And all the postmen used to get together and have a Christmas party. One of the postmen had his birthday over the Christmas period and we decorated the frame of his sorting section - each postman had a sorting section with all the boxes, to sort the mail in.

We had extra staff come in - various students and elderly people who used to go out and deliver the mail. It was always a cheerful time there. And of course going out on the rounds we used to get things given to us like Christmas cards and little gifts.

One Christmas I went along Whitefield Road and a chappie along there said, 'Oh, would you like a drink, Postman?' And he poured out this whitish liquid and I thought it was lemonade. So I drank it straight down and I remember him looking at me oddly.

I jumped on my bike, and I got down the end of the road and something hit me! I practically fell off the bike, practically took all the mail on the front of the bike with me as well. It took me probably about an hour to recover after that. I managed to find my way around and pop the letters in the letterboxes, wondering why I was feeling so terrible.

When I called on him the next day, I said, 'What on earth did you give me yesterday morning?'

'Oh, it was vodka.'

'Vodka! I've never drunk vodka in my life!'

'Oh, I thought you hadn't,' he said, 'the way you drank it down.'

*As a pupil at the Basingstoke High School, **Betty Godden** found that Christmas in the 1940s provided an opportunity for 'work experience' at the Post Office in New Street with the Christmas mail.*

Packet sorting was best. Taking one packet at a time from a large sack, one stood in front of a metal framework that was divided into many square sections, each with a sack hanging in it. Areas of the country were marked on the framework and the packet had to be thrown into the relevant section. Any packet poorly addressed was put to one side for the post office workers to decipher. Some were very inadequately addressed and we wondered if they would ever reach their destination.

We girls, and boys from the Queen Mary's Grammar School, were willing to work as many hours as asked—the first time we had been paid to work!

Robert Brown's photo of some 'casuals'

John Ferguson *got into trouble as a young boy in the 1930s.*

I remember being terribly helpful and picking up this pile of Christmas cards to post - which I duly did, only to discover that they hadn't actually got any stamps on and they had to be rescued! One interesting thing about Christmas cards was that you didn't seal the envelopes, you tucked them in. It was a brown halfpenny stamp had to go on them, and we were a bit more organised and we posted them a day or so before. Our neighbours never posted their cards until Christmas Eve and they were always delivered on Christmas morning. And that was a postal service, if you like - for a halfpenny!

Evelyn Bailey, *housekeeper at the Rectory from 1938 to 1958, received this special Christmas card from her brother . . .*

. . . and another from her employer, Archdeacon Anthony Chute.

*Micky, one of two evacuee boys at Chute House, made this card and gave it to **Evelyn** in 1939. In her diary for Thursday 21st December, she notes 'Peter & Micky gone home for Xmas. Saw them off at the Station.'*

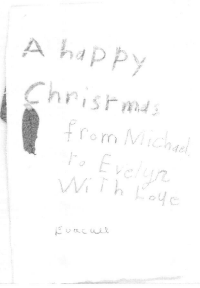

A happy Christmas from Michael to Evelyn With Love

Evacuee

Christmas cards weren't always Christmassy.

Evelyn Bailey received this card from her brother in 1935.

Owen Blissett sent this home from Iran in 1949.

Christmas 1949

Christmas Greetings and every Good Wish

for your Happiness throughout

the Coming Year

From

All Best Wishes

Owen

Royal Air Force,
Habbaniya,
M.E.A.F. 19,
Iraq.

And this card was sent to **Jo Kelly's** mother in Basingstoke by her father in Bomber Command.

With Christmas Greetings
and
Good Wishes
for
The Coming Year.

from

Billy

31

James Fitzpatrick uses local scenes for his Christmas cards today.

The Holy Ghost ruins

Deane's Almshouses

St Michael's

Church Cottage

Carols

What would Christmas be without singing carols and decorating Christmas trees? But how many carol singers today know more than one verse of 'We wish you a merry Christmas...'? And how do mechanised versions of 'Rudolph the Red-nosed Reindeer' compare with even a ragged-voiced group of singers keeping alive the old tunes and verses about the baby in the manger with the ox and ass?

Instead of opening little doors on an Advent calendar to reveal a chocolate each day, there are still some who see Advent as a solemn season when they forego chocolate and other delights. **Arthur Attwood** *describes how choirboys prepared for the festival.*

How well I remember Christmas-time when I was a boy and especially the Christmas of 1928, for I was a new choirboy at St Michael's Church, to become one of many generations to have sung in the lovely building. For choirboys, Christmas was the highlight of the year and a real climax to Advent, during which we were not allowed to sing carols, as it was not in keeping with the season.

Boys and girls went round knocking on doors, carol singing, as they do today. The only outside organised body of singers was the Salvation Army, with its band, which toured the town. In those days, you did not go shopping in the town centre to be confronted by collecting boxes with live and canned music offered, as is the case today. Neither were there the numerous carol concerts which are now commonplace in many schools.

But we choirboys did sing carols before the great festival, for we had to practise them at St John's School at a spot where the Bass House now stands. I can still picture the scene, with Mrs Anstey trying to keep us boys in order, while her blind husband endeavoured to teach us the art of singing.

Ian Murray *belonged to a group who didn't sing carols but went out ringing them on handbells.*

All Saints is the only church in the UK with nine bells and they had an unusually comprehensive set of handbells with flats and sharps. Ernie Austin, who was the Captain of the Tower, thought that it would be a good idea if we used these handbells for ringing Christmas carols. So we used to go around the area near All Saints, visiting various families, and ringing Christmas carols for them and collecting money for charity at the same time if we could. I think there must have been about six or eight of us in the group. We used to ring handbells in the same manner of changes that you do on the tower bells. But ringing for carols you had a chart - like a music chart on a music stand; each person had a number - one, two three, four and so on, and you used to follow the chart and obviously if you knew the tune it was easy enough to slot in. We did this for two or three years at Christmas time in the late 1940s.

Betty Godden *took part too.*

I enjoyed handbell ringing with the All Saints Church team. We played carols in roads near the church several evenings leading up to Christmas Day.

Deborah Woodland *describes carol-singing at St Anne's School.*

We had to put a candle in a jam jar and then the jam jar was tied to a string and the string was tied to a bamboo. And then we went out with our candles onto the playground and all stood round in a horseshoe and sang some Christmas carols. It was broad daylight so I'm not really sure what we thought we were doing!

HANTS & BERKS GAZETTE

Carol Sheet

With the Seasonal Compliments of the
Hants & Berks Gazette, Church Street, Basingstoke
Published every Friday, Price 5d.

Silent Night

Silent night! holy night!
All is calm, all is bright;
Round yon Virgin and her Child,
Holy Infant, so tender and mild,
Sleep in heavenly peace,
Sleep in heavenly peace.

Christmas trees and the crib

Mary Felgate *kept her Christmas tree candles for over sixty years.*

I remember one of the things that Miss Joice gave me, that just shows how children like something different; she gave me a little square box of Christmas candles for our Christmas tree. It was Price's Christmas Tree Candles and the illustration on the top of the box showed the candles and holly round. We did use some of the candles, but some never got used because I just kept it as a souvenir treasure, and eventually, in much later life, when I moved from my old home, I gave it to the Museum, so it must be stacked away somewhere in the Museum Service.

Michael Tarrant *had his own tree.*

My grandfather was a forester and he retired in the 1950s. Every Christmas he used to get us a Christmas tree, dig it up from somewhere. I was only eight when he died so I don't know how the Christmas trees were brought to Basingstoke, or even if my grandfather had permission to have them. I just remember that it was a bit of a tradition in the family that each year the tree belonged to one of us three children. The year he retired, just by pure luck it happened to be my tree. So we kept the tree and we planted it in the garden and we dug it up for a number of years for Christmas until it got too big. And the tree's still at the bottom of the garden now, 71 South Ham Road. It's probably a house-and-a-half high now.

Brian Butler *remembers a single bough.*

Uncle Geoffrey was very skilled when it came to decorating the tree. I remember one year when he dispensed with a tree and had a large evergreen bough suspended on wires, of course, beautifully decorated.

Jo Kelly *has a particular delight.*

. . . the smell of a real Christmas tree.

36

Hannah Williams *loved the Christmas trees at All Saints Church.*

Christmas-time in All Saints Church in the 1970s was really very special. Peter Murphy, the Vicar, always had this idea of allowing the children themselves to decorate the Christmas tree, and it didn't matter if it was a higgledy-piggledy mess of a Christmas tree, the important thing was that they did it. It is a tradition that has gone on - the youngsters always get very excited and the tree is decorated in whichever way they wished to decorate it. All Saints is a very beautiful church and when it's all lit with candles, and greenery everywhere -- well, I have very fond memories of going to church at Christmas-time with my three sons and my husband.

Deborah Woodland's *dog wasn't happy.*

I remember a small Christmas tree, when I was four, five, six. It was on a coffee table in the corner of the stairs of our house on Riverdene, and this poor tree was harassed by the dog, which didn't like it at all! My father would always be the one who would dress the tree with some   precious glass Christmas decorations that we weren't supposed to touch.

And as we got older we had a huge floor-to-ceiling white Christmas tree. Very avant-garde we were. Thinking about it now, the room must have looked quite spectacular—this would have been the mid 1960s. We had an orange carpet, orange curtains, a white three-piece suite with orange cushions and a huge white Christmas tree!

Pat Wright *describes some unique decorations.*

One year during the war we had a very, very pretty Christmas tree because the silver paper had been dropped from the aeroplanes to stop the radar and we went out and collected loads and loads of it and made all our Christmas decorations with it that year.

*Sometimes, as **Joan Bull** remembered, there was an actual forest!*

One lovely thing was the Christmas forest, which consisted of about twelve Christmas trees in a large room at St John's School in Church Street; there were many coloured lights and presents on the trees. I doubt if we were well enough off to buy presents, but we enjoyed all the colour and sparkle.

***Betty and Eric Godden** and their sons looked out for the Christmas tree and the Crib.*

Early in the 1960s a few days before 25th December, with two small sons, the family would walk through the town to see the large Christmas tree in the Market Square and along London Street to the Deane's Almshouses, in front of which was a life-size Crib, setting the scene of Christmas.

*As a child, **Deborah Woodland** was fascinated by the Crib.*

In the middle of the front garden outside the Deane's Almshouses there was always a floral display of a clock or a pattern, but it was always removed at Christmas and replaced with a Nativity scene. That used to fascinate me, I could stand there for hours and look at it. So we always had to take a detour when we were shopping so that I could go and stand and look at it. I suppose the little stable construction must have been wood, and I remember straw on the bottom. I don't know what the actual characters would have been made of, it must have been something durable. To my little eyes the stable must have been quite big, perhaps six foot high or something like that, a substantial thing.

Some of the Christmas displays in Basingstoke's Festival Place are simply secular.

38

Jessie Jack, *known to many as Sister Wilcox, describes how the Shrubbery Maternity Home was decorated.*

When I first came to the Shrubbery it was June in 1947 but the Shrubbery itself had opened in November 1946. Old Mr Cooper had been the gardener when it was a private house - and he was a great man, he really was. At Christmas time he used to come with his wife and help to decorate and it was a lovely house to decorate because it was wooden panels and in the hall there was a lovely wrought iron fire with a copper hood. Oh, it was beautiful. We did all the ward but they did the hall, the dining-room and the clinic and that.

Barbara Green, *a nurse at the Cottage Hospital in Hackwood Road in the 1950s, compares arrangements then and now.*

Another thing we used to do at Christmas, we used to make sure the hospital was full. Not empty, full. So that people who were poor could have a good Christmas; and little children, especially those that were poor, were going to have a good time. We used to make sure they came in, and they had lovely food, and happiness, and presents. That was another thing. Now they try to keep them empty, of course. You mustn't be ill at Christmas now.

*In the Second World War the **Canadian Hospital** at Hackwood Park decorated their Sergeants' Mess for Christmas.*

Plays and Concerts

In 1948 **Betty Godden** *took part in a wonderful Nativity play, with beautiful costumes and imaginative staging.*

The curate in charge of All Saints, Rev Ronald Wynne, produced an ambitious Nativity play with mainly adult performers from St Michael's as well as All Saints.

Wearing long white robes and enormous arm-length wings, I remember having to make an elevated entrance by precariously walking over wooden beer crates piled in the choir stalls!

The previous evening at the Twenties Club Will Ferguson, who had been a PTI in the RAF, had given us an evening of Physical Exercises. Now, as an angel, having to walk down the centre aisle of All Saints Church and genuflect to the ground with wings outstretched, all the stiff muscles protested.

Margaret Evans *made the wings for the archangels.*

I was detailed to make all these wings, make the frame with buckram and then cut out small pieces of crepe paper to look like feathers and stick them onto the buckram and gradually build up a wing for each of the men.

Owen Blissett *still meets Mary today, after more than seventy years.*

It must have been when I was about seven that I played Joseph in the Congregational Church Christmas Nativity play; my 'wife', the Virgin Mary still lives in Basingstoke and we occasionally bump into each other and have a laugh about old times.

As a child **Deborah Woodward** *wasn't satisfied with the scripts for school Nativity plays.*

As for the annual Nativity play, couldn't it be a bit more grown-up with more words so that anyone who didn't know the story could find out?

Beryl Northcott *taught at Cliddesden Village School in the 1930s.*

At Christmas we always had to produce a Christmas Concert and of course all the parents came - that was a great day. One year we had it down in the village hall in Cliddesden in the evening. Then it wasn't a Nativity Play but 'Christopher Robin is saying his prayers'. I think I made up the words and got someone to make up the music for me. I had the children dressed in night dresses and carrying candles and they sang. Christopher Robin was kneeling at the bed and the other children came in carrying their candles and singing this little song, 'Tip tip toe, tip tip toe, creeping up to bed we go,' and then they stood around him and he recited 'Christopher Robin is saying his prayers'. Then I think there was another little song and they went off. It was quite successful - but then, of course, the parents, with children at that age, they love it whatever they do, don't they!

It was difficult each year to try and think of something new. The first Christmas I was there, when it was all new to me, I wasn't very good at it. Another teacher lent me a song about poppies in golden corn and it was really quite effective and I made them little red crêpe paper skirts so that they were in red.

Arthur Attwood *commented on the report of the Nativity Play at Queen Mary's School in 1946.*

The Christmas season was celebrated by a presentation of a Nativity Play, *The Child in Flanders*, by Cicely Hamilton. The story of the Annunciation, the Shepherds, the Manger and the Three Kings was told by means of tableaux on the stage, accompanied by carols, recitative, and orchestra music from performers grouped in the gallery. The enduring relevance of the Bethlehem story was indicated in the Prologue and the Epilogue, played and spoken from the stage by Dudley Keep, Ernest Crutchley and Shivaji Lal as an English, Australian and Indian soldier in the 1914-18 war, and by Roger Willis as a French peasant, who gives them shelter on Christmas Eve. The birth of a son that night to the Frenchman and his wife, and the gifts made to the child by the three strangers, gave a modern parallel to the centuries-old story.

Catherine Metcalfe *(then Cathy Abbott) took part in St John's School's Christmas play in 1952, aged 9 years, 4 months. She was Mrs Cratchett (second from left, second row).*

Jo Kelly *was in the Coombehurst School's Nativity Play in 1953.*

Yes, I am the angel with my eyes open.

Paul Connolly *was the first headmaster of Bishop Challoner School when it opened in 1975.*

We began with a first year only of intake and I was determined from the start to make music a feature of school life. I set myself to do a music concert at Christmas and to make sure that every child in the school was involved. Every child was in the choir, 120 youngsters, and various people did readings and little dramas. And it got the atmosphere and spirit of the school off to a good start. Also a couple of days before that we had a big party and about 250 people came and the staff organised games and activities and entertainment.

*Paul's wife, **Anne**, remembers more music-making.*

At Christmas in particular Paul and I would go round various places and sing, old folks' homes and little concerts and the old folk would join in. Now I've joined the Ladies' Choir and we always do a Christmas concert for the old folks, we get invited to all sorts of different groups to go and sing around Christmas time. We sing at the Mayor's Charity Christmas Concert. The Male Voice Choir, the Ladies' Choir and the Hurst Choir are always there to sing and they have different people doing solos.

Hannah Williams *once organised some special carol singing.*

The Horseshoe Theatre, Basingstoke's professional theatre company at the Haymarket, put on a production of Charles Dickens's *A Christmas Carol*. It was soon after the company had been formed and, as they needed to get audiences, I came up with the idea of getting different choirs, holding lanterns and wearing bobble caps, to sing carols outside the theatre as people were coming in. The play was on for about a fortnight

and I managed to get the Salvation Army Band there one night, the choir from All Saints Church another night, school choirs and groups of singers from several local choirs. And don't think that they all went in afterwards on free tickets, because they didn't! And the result was that *A Christmas Carol* was virtually a sell-out on that first production in 1977.

We've done *A Christmas Carol* three times over the last 36 years. I've seen all three of them but it is that first one that really stays in my memory. Daniel Slater, the son of the producer, was about six years of age at the time. He was slightly built, growing quite tall, and just about right really to play Tiny Tim.

John Dinan invariably brought out his accordion at Christmas parties at the Shrubbery (which the Horseshoe Theatre Company used for rehearsals), so Guy Slater decided that John would play carols

on his accordion on stage for this production, dressed in Victorian costume. Oh, and how he loved that! He did look magnificent.

Christmas parties

Brian Spicer, who was the Estate Agent for Lord Camrose, describes arrangements for parties at Hackwood House. It was the first Viscount Camrose who started the parties in 1936 and they were continued by the second Viscount (except for the War years) until 1994.

Lord Camrose and his family used to have their own Christmas festivities early and they would put up a large Christmas tree in the hall. It was brought in from the forest, the full height of the hall, over 25 feet. Then they used to go to a hotel in Switzerland for Christmas, leaving the Christmas tree up for the two staff parties.

The butler, chef, housekeeper and kitchen staff organised a party for the outside staff and the house staff, with the dining room table laid for 34. Then some of the people who had been guests at that party organised another for the kitchen staff.

Jean Chivers used to enjoy the Hackwood parties. She came to Hackwood Park in 1978 when her husband became a gardener.

The Christmas party was an old tradition. All the house staff were invited, and the staff that worked on the grounds. I think the farm had their own separate celebration. We all had a proper invitation, and we had to answer it or we didn't go. So we answered it straight away.

Lady Camrose would have the tables all beautifully decorated, and the chef used to make the lovely meals. I remember the first couple of years it was a hot meal, but after that it became more of a buffet, so you went to help yourself. There was salmon one year, and there was always loads of prawns, and a cold meat platter, the chef used to do it so beautifully. And then we would have, perhaps, a fruit salad, or there were big trifles with loads and loads of cream on. And there was loads of wine - I don't drink anything, but there was lemonade, so I would have a drink of lemonade. But there was plenty there if anybody wanted anything.

Then, after we had had our meal, we didn't have to do anything, we just walked away and left it all, and we went down into the cinema, and we had a film.

That was in the house, a lovely old cinema. It wasn't very large, but there was lines of cane chairs, little tables with ash trays on them, all crystal, beautiful, and at the back there was an old settee. So we used to try and sit in this old settee, because it was really comfortable. And the film was usually 007s, James Bond. I think Lord Camrose must have had a thing about James Bond, because we had a lot of his films, even before they had come out in the cinema. He used to have them sent down from London for us specially. So that was nice. We did see *The Thirty-nine Steps* once, and another one about a black horse, made in Sardinia. That one was beautiful. Lady Camrose's family got part of Sardinia.

If you didn't want to go down there, you could stop upstairs and have a dance, but I always used to go down in the cinema and watch that. The dancing was to tapes, but they had someone playing piano one year. We had the run of the house. They used to say, 'Have a good time'.

And up they used to go and you didn't see them again. You could go anywhere you wanted, but you didn't do that because it's not your house. It was a lovely old house.

We had Christmas presents, but I think they came through the housekeeper from Lady Camrose. The first year I had a sewing box and I've used that one ever since. We had some beautiful Irish lace mats, one time. I still use those. Tablemats, beautiful lacy ones, and serviettes, and tablecloth to match and everything. One year was premium bonds. And Sainsbury's vouchers you had every year, which were really useful. And there was always a Christmas pudding, some mince-pies. The cook used to make mince-pies: so many were given to each of us. And you had a bottle of wine as well. And we always had two pheasants off the keeper. So we had a really good time at Christmas. They looked after us very well. I was just sorry it couldn't have gone on for a bit longer.

Harold Gates _at Hackwood wanted his pheasant._

I worked in the dairy on the Hackwood Estate until I was called up in World War 2. I didn't go back into the dairy when I came back, I went out on the farm, tractor driving. And it was quite interesting to see people's reaction to me. They all knew me as a boy, the farm manager used to call me 'lad'. 'Arr lad, while I think of it, you do so and so and so and so', you see. And when I came back at 26 years old they still treated me as a lad, you know what I mean! It's surprising isn't it? They say, 'Go away a boy and come back a man,' and it was true in this case. At Christmas time each worker, forestry, farm, or what, would be given a pheasant as a present. Well, my father had one and at the time there was a father and son working on the forestry and they had a pheasant each but of course I didn't get one. They said, 'Well, you're not married, are you?' I said, 'What! What difference does that make?'

And anyway I got my pheasant after an argument, and that was that.

Nita Abbott *worked at Park Prewett Hospital in the mid 1960s*

Miss Orchard used to organise wonderful Christmas parties, and the electricians and everybody would give their time, and the marvellous lights they had up, the decorations they did, all in their own time. I remember once there was a small train went weaving in and out at the back of the hall. We all came away with a brown paper bag full of goodies, apples and oranges.

Catherine Metcalfe *enjoyed them as a child about 1945.*

The first Christmas I remember was when I was about four years old, in a pink knitted dress, on the corner of a large photograph of a children's party at the hospital. At that time there were perhaps 100 to 150 children being entertained in the large Hall at the hospital.

Catherine is in the front row, left. Her father had just brought the family to Basingstoke when patients were being moved back into Park Prewett, so she didn't know anyone and felt rather lost.

The next year she also went to a party of the Wellington Club, for children of staff at Park Prewett. Catherine is the one with her fingers in her mouth; on her right is Catherine Constadine, then Judy and Geoffrey Passingham. Behind them was Mrs Green 'who managed everything'.

Joan Bull *used to go to parties at the Town Hall, which is now the Willis Museum.*

Families that were hard up could get tickets for the children for Christmas Parties held at the Town Hall. Food consisted of bread & butter, cakes and brightly coloured jellies. We played games and they sometimes had a magician.

So did **Peggy Barker.**

The Town Hall was the centre of life really. I can remember as a small girl, the great thing was at Christmas they always had a party there in aid of Barnardos and they always had a conjurer, and the excitement of getting dressed up and going to the Town Hall in Basingstoke. Oh, I can't tell you, it was amazing and it was incredibly well done.

*Firms organised children's parties too, as **Bob Applin** explains.*

For children whose fathers worked at Thornycrofts, the Christmas party in the Canteen was an eagerly awaited event in the weeks leading up to Christmas, usually held on the Saturday before Christmas. Hundreds of us could not wait for the afternoon to arrive. I think it was for a restricted age range - from memory, five- to ten-year-olds.

The party always had the same format when I went, between 1947 and 1950, and it ran from three o'clock to seven. Mr 'Roly' Edwards was the compère - he talked 'POSH'. The first half was a film show - black and white Disney cartoons and Popeye, followed by tea provided by the ladies of the Canteen staff. Sandwiches - I forget what fillings - jelly and cake, and squash to drink.

Then back to the main hall for more entertainment. I think there was always a conjurer and then a 'Talent Show', when we were invited onto the stage to perform - some brave souls did. One girl's effort sticks in my mind. There was a popular song at the time, using the alphabet: 'A you're adorable, B you're so beautiful' etc. She went on stage to sing this and started confidently, but by M or thereabouts her memory failed and a very red-faced and crestfallen young lady retired hurriedly from the stage. This took things up to the arrival of Father Christmas and distribution of presents from his sack. Always something quite small and simple - I remember getting a comb one year.

However, my strongest memory is not of the party but of being able to take a close and leisurely look at the exhibition engines that were stored in the Canteen. Beautiful polished, painted and chrome-plated full-size engines cut in half lengthways to show the internal details. These were used at motor shows etc. Although I never became an engineer, I am sure seeing the engines started my life-long interest in technology.

50

Christmas toys

Snow shaker
D2006.5

D1998.457

Speed boat given by
Mary Felgate

HCMS 1968.662

More Christmas toys

Bonzo

HCMS 1969.660

Japanese water flowers

ACM 1968.201

Old Daddy Tin-whiskers

BWM 1965.597

Pop gun D200.37

St Michael's at Christmas
Anita Leatherby

Hospital pantos

Deborah Woodland's *mother worked at Eli Lilly and her father at Thornycrofts so she remembers children's parties at both firms.*

I remember going into Lilly's, the big white building, when I was around five, six, or seven. It must have been the canteen, because long thin tables were laid out and my sister and I would sit together. Lots of our school friends were at these parties as well, because their parents too worked for Eli Lilly's. We had red jelly, which stained everything in sight! And big jugs of orange squash.

I remember my silver glittery party shoes and my party dress, pale blue with little white flowers on it and a skirt underneath and net over the top with a big bow on it. And my sister had a yellow one. My grandmother had knitted us white lacy cardigans to go with them. All the girls had party dresses. Two of my friends from primary school actually turned up wearing the same thing but in a different colour. We thought this was marvellous! All the little boys would turn up in their bow ties and make sure their socks were pulled up. The rule at school was that boys would wear shorts, so this was a big day in a little boy's life, to wear trousers!

I remember a lady at a Thornycrofts party trying to get everybody to sit down for 'Pass the Parcel'. Lots of the little children didn't want to leave their parents, so this circle was getting bigger and bigger. I remember this parcel coming round, which was so huge that the children could barely handle it and as it got passed round you couldn't see people, they lost themselves behind it.

The older children were allowed to play 'Musical chairs' but the little ones didn't, probably because we might have hurt ourselves.

There was some dancing as well, and we seem to have spent an awful lot of time at parties singing 'Yellow Submarine'!

Deborah says that Father Christmas obviously got around quite a bit. She and her sister Gillian went to see him at the Co-op every year.

At the Thornycroft parties you had to go up onto a stage to go and see Father Christmas and I remember being not at all happy because all the children's names were read out and as your name was called you went and received your present, and then a Diane Woodland was called, and I thought, 'Well, my name's not Diane,' so I didn't go. And it wasn't until afterwards that the organisers realised that they had got the name wrong, and so this poor lady had to come and find me and take me to Father Christmas because the name was wrong on the present. It was something furry, I think it must have been a teddy or something.

DECEMBER 22 1883

SALVATION ARMY

Several friends are coming for Christmas.

On Christmas Eve our Fruit Banquet;

Christmas morning, at 7, breakfast;
meetings at 11 o'clock and 6.30;

Boxing Day, a great Tea at 4 o'clock,
tickets 8d each:

harmonious meeting at 7.

The family comes

Mary Felgate had happy childhood memories, in the early 1920s.

My Christmas really began when Grandpa and Grandma arrived from Dorking and Grandma's large ninepenny Book of Carols was on the open piano and Grandpa's violin case was down by the piano. Dad always allowed a fire in the front room. Mother gave me the job of arranging all the cushions on the hearthrug so as to warm them and get rid of any damp. Many happy times were spent round the piano, Grandma playing, Grandpa accompanying on his violin and the four of us gathered round to sing carols.

Do you remember Zuzzas? Metal tubes with something in the end, by which you zuzzed the carol tunes when all round the piano. Others had tissue or paper over a comb, and that made the same sort of noise.

I well remember my infant astonishment when Mother carried me into the dining room a few days before Christmas, and it was completely decorated with paper chains from the centre gas light to the corners of the room. Paper chains were draped round the large overmantle and over the top of the ornamental headboard above the immense mirror of the sideboard. There were holly sprays behind every picture on the walls (and there were a great many pictures in those days), and silver stars with angel scrap pictures in the middle of them, hanging on various places. I also remember asking how the decorations got there, and Mother told me the fairies did the decorations in the night, and I was absolutely enchanted by it.

On the top of the oak shelf over the mirror overmantle over the fireplace, there was a small Father Christmas, with a very jolly little face and cotton wool beard, but I was rather terrified of him, as I knew he would be the one to bring his sack in the night and fill our long black stockings hung on the bedposts, and I

D20002.51

53

was afraid he might make a mistake and grow big and come down off the shelf during the day, and I did not want to see him grown-up size. I never had any ambition to see him come into the bedroom with his sack, as some children wished to see.

Then later I remember being taken into the front room where there was the Christmas tree decorated. That was a great delight, hung with presents and candles that were clipped on in those days with metal clips.

John Ashlin *says one year Christmas was sent **from** Basingstoke!*

Christmas 1957, I was a young policeman in London. I was married with an 11-month-old baby. I was very poorly paid and we frequently could not afford a day's food. I had to walk four miles to work and back, as I did not have the bus fare. Christmas dinner was scheduled to be a stew and we had no money for presents or decorations; to be in debt was to be sacked.

My wife and I both had family in Basingstoke and my sister lived in London. We were too proud to tell anyone that we were so desperately poor and we had little communication with family; no-one had a phone.

Then out of the blue Betty's mum and sister appeared with Christmas puddings, mince pies and other Christmas goodies. My mum sent us a goose. My sister appeared and, seeing no decorations, went out and bought us some decorations, a little Christmas tree, some half bottles of wine and miniature brandy, chocolates etc. There were presents for us and the baby and suddenly we had a Christmas! It was like the Cratchets had in *A Christmas Carol*. We have had many good Christmases since then but none better or more memorable.

Christmas Eve

Ethel Lizzie Moody's diary, 1895, when she was 21.

> 24 *Tuesday*
> *Cooking all morning - shopping in the afternoon & decorating after tea. Frank and Harry Clift came home by the mail train. Had Snapdragon in the dining-room.*

Snapdragon was a Victorian game traditionally played during the Christmas season. A shallow bowl was filled with brandy, raisins were tossed in and the brandy set on fire.

Players tried to snatch raisins from the flickering blue flames and pop them, still burning, into their mouths! The burning raisins were called snapdragons.

As a child in the 1920s **Ruby Philpott** *was buying Christmas presents at the last minute.*

Christmas Eve was a great time. In those days the shops weren't all decorated until about six weeks before Christmas, and I used to go out and buy my Christmas presents on Christmas Eve, using the pocket money I'd saved up (3d a week and 6d to put on a saving stamp). I used to go up Wote Street to Bucklands and buy something like a fancy blotter for my Father, and then I'd go into Kemps and buy a handkerchief for my Mother, or a lace collar for my sisters. It was very simple in those days.

Diana Stanley in her book **Within Living Memory** *describes an old tradition on Christmas Eve.*

Many people can remember seeing the gypsies camping on the grass verges of Pack Lane, before the 1914-18 war. On Christmas Eve they used to visit some of the cottages where they were known and welcomed. The cottage folk might be expecting them as in previous years, but they never heard a sound until there was a rustling of footsteps in the porch. Then the singing began; not joyous Christmas carolling but a strange Oriental kind of dirge - the music of the true Romanies with their Indian heritage nearly a thousand years old.

Remember, friends, that we are made of clay,
And in this world we have not long to stay...

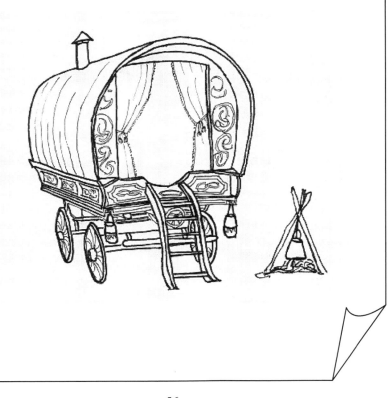

The same thoughts were expressed in **The Manual,** *a devotional book given to* **Judy Melluish's** *grandmother,* **Elizabeth Beale** *on 4th May 1885 by Canon J E Millard, Vicar of Basingstoke (co-author of* **The History of Basingstoke**). *It gave the following advice for Advent, the Church's preparation for Christmas.*

1   Bear any trouble, or do any hard work, or receive any pleasure, with little care, saying to thyself, *It is not long. Christ cometh quickly.*

2   Think, speak and act, remembering the Judgment Day.

3   If thou art awake in the night, or when thou liest down in the dark, say,
The son of Man cometh as a thief in the night.
At midnight there was a cry made, "The Bridegroom cometh".

John Arlott *describes a Basingstoke street scene in 1921.*

It was almost upon us. Griffin the butcher's traps, with their high-stepping ponies, moved through the streets on their delivery rounds, more arrogantly, at increasing pace and later into the evening. The postmen seemed to be delivering from morning to night.

I still retain a picture in mind, a single vignette. A tiny flurry of snow, lit yellow by a street gas-lamp and an old lady with a black bonnet, short coat and long black skirt pausing in the moment before she crossed the road, a bundle of firewood under one arm, two bottles under the other; a coal cart ground slowly by, the coalman, a sprig of mistletoe in his hat, leant boozily towards her - 'Got a kiss for us, Meg?' - 'Wash your old face first,' she shouted and went cackling on her way.

Betty Godden *talks of last minute baking.*

With no fridges or freezers in the 50s, one remembers working late on Christmas Eve making mince pies and other fancies before brushing off the flour to go to Midnight Mass at All Saints Church.

Deborah Woodland's *family were on the move.*

Every Christmas Eve used to be spent driving around Middlesex to go and visit all my father's brothers and sisters and their families to exchange presents. I think that was a very clever move on the part of my mum and dad because that meant we were so tired in the car on the way home we fell asleep, so we could just be put to bed.

Neil Ogden *talks about preparations for the special Christmas schedule for* **Hospital Radio Basingstoke.**

For two or three weeks over Christmas we have extra live programmes and events and recorded shows.

For The Great Christmas Cracker Bash we go round the wards and pull crackers on air with staff and patients. We also run a competition when we give away tickets to the local pantos and shows. And then on Christmas morning we do a similar thing live from as many parts of the hospital as we can get to in two hours.

Christmas has not been without its technical problems, though. A couple of years ago I walked in on Christmas Eve in the morning and the hard drive on the computer had died the previous evening.

But, thanks to a member of Hospital Radio Reading, who happens to run a computer shop in Newbury, we spent that afternoon getting it back up and running and we were able to do our Christmas shows as planned.

Christmas Day

How early did Christmas Day begin? And did you have a real woollen stocking, a decorative one, a pillowcase or a sack?

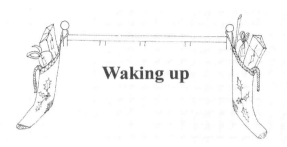

Waking up

Mary Felgate had a stocking in about 1916.

The most exciting moment of Christmas was the early morning, probably about 5 o'clock, when it was still dark. My brother and I, still very young, slept in the front bedroom. I slept in my cot with high railing sides, against the wall near the window, and he slept in the big double bed with iron frame, and end posts with brass knobs, and in between them square brass rods which I loved to turn round and round, as they squeaked.

When we awoke, the two long black woollen stockings were hanging on a string loop on the two ends of the big bed. Mine, of course, was my side, where I could feel and reach it from my cot. It was very thrilling to feel the little parcels through the stocking and try and guess the contents. We knew we were not allowed to take the stockings down and undo the presents until it was light enough to see, and I am sure we both fell asleep again until the daylight came.

Then what a rustling and delving into the depth of the very long stockings! The little parcels came out one by one, and were opened and compared with each other. I don't remember the many things there were in the stockings, but I do know there was always an apple or orange or mandarin somewhere inside, and the toe of my stocking always had the expected packet containing one pink sugar mouse and one white sugar mouse, each with a pink nose and a string tail.

I always nibbled the nose of one mouse, and sometimes the whole head, and saved the string tail end until later. Then I carefully wrapped each parcel up again, and put them all back into the stocking, to be kept until the afternoon, when the rest of the family came for tea, to show to the Aunties who came up from the Church Street shop. This practice of putting the parcels back into the stocking used to infuriate my little brother, and he used to complain to Mother about it. He thought I was stupid. But it was an enjoyment to be renewed as I undid each parcel again to show to my Aunties.

I also remember one occasion when my brother disobeyed and undid one of his parcels in the flickering light from the tiny blue gas jet which was always left alight all night for us, and he had a small painting book and a packet of greasy-type crayons, and he started to colour some of the pictures of soldiers and sailors. I teased him when it was daylight as he could not possibly have seen the colours of the crayons in the gaslight, and he had got lots of colours wrong. The packet of crayons had a picture of a rising sun with radiating sunbeams on the outside. Once my stocking held a lovely little settee and two armchairs, made of cardboard and covered with chintz, which my Mother had made for me for the dolls' house.

One Christmas when I woke up Mother showed me an enormous (to me) box at the foot of the bed, from Father Christmas, which, when opened, held a complete set of china dolls' cups and saucers. A wonderful present to me, as it was a huge box for Father Christmas to have brought down the chimney!

Mary Felgate *gave these toys to the Willis Museum.*

D1987.21

D1989.39

BWM 1968.75

Brian Butler *remembers the 1920s*

Ah, the ritual of putting a pillow case and a sock at the end of the bed and then the early morning rummage - and always a tangerine in the heel of the sock!

John Arlott *remembers 1921.*

Some inbuilt emotional control must have adjusted the almost unbearable excitement so that it reached its just-containable peak by bed-time on Christmas Eve, and allowed it to subside to the brink of sleep an hour before the presents were put softly beside the bed. There they were in the morning - not morning, really - still night - explored first with groping hand and then! look at the rest with *my own* electric torch - at all the impossible presents - how did they *know*? Open-mouthed through all those weeks to that final heady morning - such a morning as has left many of us striving ever since, through the dim, almost perverse, inarticulate failure of children, to utter the adequate 'Thank you' for the actuality—and the recollection—of it.

And **Arthur Attwood** *remembers 1928.*

For us children, as is the case today, it all began in the early hours when we looked for and found a stocking. The contents were much different, for there were novelties that could be bought for a few coppers. A bar of Caley's chocolate bought for a penny, sugar mice, squeakers, doll's house kitchen utensils made of tin, toy trumpets, etc.

The old iron bedsteads were much more serviceable for hanging up the stockings, but, alas, few of us had an electric light to switch on, we either had a paraffin lamp or candles. If we had the latter, there was the warning from Mum and Dad about being careful. The candle would flicker and one would watch the candlegrease forming in the candlestick. Candles were also used for the Christmas tree and again we were told to be careful.

Deborah Woodland *enjoyed waking up.*

There were all the presents that had magically turned up in the house while we were asleep. My sister's would always be put across one of the white armchairs and mine would always be put across the other white armchair - and it looked like thousands of things! There was always a Christmas stocking and, both being girls, there was always hand cream or bubble bath or something like that. And the obligatory selection box with the variety of chocolates in it.

Jo Kelly *did well!*

I was an only child and knew I was spoilt. I had a sack at the bottom of my bed as well as a stocking!

Ruby Philpott's *breakfast was rather unusual.*

We always had lots and lots of visitors come to stay for Christmas, and we used to get up and look at our presents in our stockings. Then we'd have - oh, this must sound funny to you - we'd have haddock for breakfast, yellow haddock, London cured.

In the 1930s ***John Ferguson's*** *grandmother had her own speciality.*

My Mother's mother, who lived at the other end of Basingstoke, used to join us. I have vivid memories of my Mother doing most of the cooking for Christmas Day, but Grandmama's particular thing was the bread sauce for the turkey, and she used to get up at about six o'clock in the morning and make this bread sauce and then sit by the stove. She used to cook it on the coke water heater boiler - you simply lifted the lid off, put the saucepan on the top there and cooked away. She was there the whole morning, stirring this bread sauce.

Presents

Mary Felgate and her brother had interesting presents.

One year Grandma Langdon brought me a baby doll in long clothes. How I loved him! I called him Edward, after the Prince of Wales, and I remember being asked how I knew the doll was a boy, and I said he looked like one, and they laughed. On one occasion when I was older, a rag doll was sent me by a friend of Mother's, and I was so indignant about it, as I had long got past the rag doll stage.

We often had a shared present. One was a white elephant with a blue riding cover on his back edged with a gold ribbon. A great favourite, but in the end he was rather squashed and his legs went out sideways, as we used to sit on him and pretend we were riding it.

Either I or my brother had a Bulldog printing outfit and we made great use of it together. On the cover there was a brightly coloured picture of John Bull with a red white and blue waistcoat and a British bulldog sitting beside him. You slotted all the little tiny rubber letters onto a piece of wood and made up your words, and you pressed them into the inking pad and then you could print the words onto the paper, and we used to write little letters to our friends. One year my little friend Barbara was given a very small tin toy typewriter, and the letters on those were on a circular piece of metal with the rubber letters underneath, and you turned them round with your finger and pressed each letter in turn. We used to write letters on that too.

Some more of the dolls and toys Mary gave to the Museum.

BWM 1965.29

ACM 1968.218

BWM 1065.686

Geoffrey Butler had a generous aunt in the 1920s.

When Uncle Jim came down to Fairholme (from Bushy Park) Auntie Annie always came too, carrying her little Pekinese dog under her arm and a big handbag. She always gave us children half-a-crown and just before Christmas huge parcels full of toys would come by post from Harrods or Gamages, big stores in London. I had soldiers and all sorts of presents. I think she liked me best. As I got older Auntie Annie's presents became more expensive. Things like Hornby trains, Meccano and steam engines. Meccano became my favourite. I was fascinated by assembling and building. I saved all my pennies to buy more parts until I had a huge collection which included a Meccano clockwork motor which cost 7s 6d. I also had a Bowman stationary steam engine. I made a model of the Eiffel Tower and a Big Wheel with ten cars which I made on the fretwork machine. Finally I made a trailer with 33 rubber-tyred wheels geared down with the clockwork motor. I could sit on the trailer and the motor would pull me along.

John Ferguson was also happy to get Meccano in the 1930s.

I was a tremendous fan of Meccano and I always hoped for that for Christmas, and often got it. We also had something which nowadays I can only compare to something like Lego. It was called Bakko, and you could build houses with steel rods and slide the bricks in between.

My parents did us very well, but what we looked forward to was the mysterious parcel that came from Exeter, from my Father's mother and his elder sister and younger brother.

But at the same time Graham Kirby found some presents didn't last very long.

I got a humming top which you pushed and it spun around - and that probably lasted me about two or three days. And my sister got a little plastic dolly, where the legs were held on by elastic bands and the arms, and the head. Of course that lasted about three days. But then, that was the way everybody else was. Nobody had anything so we were quite happy really.

Betty Godden's *family did things rather differently one year.*

My first memory of Christmas in Basingstoke must have been in 1935. I lived in Junction Road, which was very near the station, so that my father, who had recently completed 22 years in the Navy could commute to his new position in the City. As we were virtually in transit from Portsmouth before moving to New Malden in the suburbs, Christmas was slightly subdued. Instead of family presents on a Christmas tree we had a Bran Tub, each taking a dip for a present.

Deborah Woodland *was luckier.*

I think I was about eleven when I got the dolls' house. Before that my sister and I were a bit tomboyish and we had garages and forts and that sort of thing. My father was a Grenadier Guard, so that's where forts and soldiers came in. I was absolutely delighted with one fort. I played with it for hours! It was creamy-yellow, with foliage painted on the side and a drawbridge and all the rest of it. And you could even pull the little soldiers apart!

John Ashlin *was an evacuee from Portsmouth, whose mother set up a guest house in Basingstoke's May Place. He thinks quality is better than quantity when it comes to Christmas presents.*

I said to my grandchildren yesterday, when we were sorting out their toys, that any one of them had more toys than children in a row of houses would have had. Well, I had one toy one Christmas, I'm not bemoaning my fate, I'm just stating a fact, it's as things were. I had a tin helmet which I thought was a wonderful one, I could play soldiers. And a book. But that was Christmas - oh, and I'd have some new piece of clothing, I'd have a new jumper, or a pair of gloves, or something like this, always a piece of clothing. I didn't feel deprived or hard done to because everybody else was the same. Some kids got a few bits more but mostly you didn't get an awful lot.

Mary Fraser *tells of her presents in the late 1930s.*

As a small child I had dolls given to me, which were largely ignored in favour of books. Father Christmas usually bought one or two of these plus pencils etc. and once a two-wheeled fairy cycle.

Ethel Lizzie Moody's *diary, 1895.*

25 Wednesday
Had 17 cards & 6 presents. Went to Church in the morning. Willie Cannon came in to tea. Went to hear carols in the evening.

Arthur Attwood *tells how, as a member of St Michael's Choir, he was always kept busy on Christmas Day in the late 1920s.*

On the great day, we would be expected to sing at the 10 a.m. Children's Service, 11 a.m. Matins and, in the afternoon, at the Basingstoke Cottage Hospital at Hackwood Road, where we would be entertained to tea.

The Church, however, like every other facet of life, has changed today with greatest changes brought about during the past ten years. No longer do church folk walk through the darkened streets to attend Holy Communion at 6.15 a.m. with other celebrations at 7, 8 and 12 noon on Christmas Day. There was no Midnight Mass, although this had been pioneered by All Saints Church since the 1920s. Instead of Family Communion at 10 a.m., as we have today, there would be Matins at 11 a.m., and it was quite usual for people to come into the town from the villages to worship in what is the pro-cathedral of North Hampshire.

*. . . and so was his son **Robin** in 1957.*

Like my father, I was a choir boy and remember singing at St Michael's on Christmas morning and in the afternoon going up to the Hackwood Road Hospital to sing carols to the patients. Archdeacon Chute led the choir and the patients would join in. Then all the choirboys would tuck in to a fantastic tea.

Joan Bull *remembers that the Salvation Army were busy too.*

The Salvation Army used to go round singing carols and people invited them in for cups of tea.

On Christmas morning there was the thrill of the postman's knock as he delivered his last letters and, sometimes, a bigger thrill, when the parcel post arrived. Postal deliveries on Christmas morning were taken for granted.

. . . *and* **Robert Brown** *delivered it.*

One Christmas Day two of us had to go out to a cul-de-sac in Oakley to deliver some parcels - in those days we used to deliver on Christmas Day. We had a parcel for every house in that cul-de-sac, so the driver put his fist onto the hooter, **Berp, Berp, Berp**, and everybody came running out, saying 'What's going on? What's going on?' And we handed out these parcels to the various occupants.

*As **Irene Compton** remarks, the nurses at The Shrubbery Maternity Home were at work too.*

The staff would normally have to work quite a long day. We didn't get any time off during Christmas Day. You were expected to go in in the morning and you handed over then to the night staff. There was no split shifts and changing, so you really didn't have a Christmas for yourself until you got home, which could be at 8 o'clock at night if the night staff were coming on then.

*But **Jessie Jack**, who delivered so many babies there, says that everyone enjoyed it.*

We used to have a great time and we all used to arrive on duty on Christmas morning to have breakfast together and we used to give Matron her communal present and she used to give us all little individual ones. All the patients had presents, and the babies; and then all day long we were entertaining the patients really. If we were busy with deliveries of babies, well then, you know, we did what we could.

Early in the morning, say, about ten-ish, the doctors used to come, not particularly to do rounds but to come and see the patients and wish them a Merry Christmas, and they'd bring their children - oh, it was great. And then the Salvation Army used to come. If it was a nice morning, sunny and crisp, they would be out on the lawn to play Christmas carols and the patients would have a whip round for them. If it was raining they'd come into the hall and there was a sort of a well there you looked up, and there was a sort of a balustrade where the patients who were up and about used to stand watching them and when they'd finished we used to give them mince pies and coffee, or squash, whatever they wanted.

At dinner time one of the doctors, Dr Bowen-Jones, used to come and carve the turkey. And in the afternoon the patients could have as many visitors as they wished and we gave them all tea. Well, it was murder at times because children came, but Matron was very understanding, they used to sit on the beds and run around but they all had tea with their mums and dads, whoever had come to visit them. Cook always made a gorgeous cake.

Hazel Montague-Ebbs *told us that the traditions continued when the Maternity Home moved up to the 'Mini Hospital' in Aldermaston Road in 1969.*

Christmas was a very important time, and very special, because most of the GPs would come in during the course of the morning, have a cup of coffee, and they would have family members with them. The Christmas Day Baby would always be given a gift, sometimes knitted by the staff, whether it was a jacket, booties. And then Christmas lunch for those few that were in hospital. It was always a time to try and get everybody home, to be with their families, but obviously at times there were people there and we always had a Christmas lunch that was sent up from the main kitchens and I believe that one of the GPs actually plated the lunch to give to the patients. We always liked the patients to be in the Day room, not to have their meals in bed, and so it was always decorated very nicely - Christmas tree, lights, cards. A very special time for staff and patients.

Sylvia North *gives more details.*

One year I dressed up as Father Christmas and when we woke the mums up (about 6 am or 5.30) we gave them a little present for the babies. Then we had to get the mums up to sit on bedpans and be swabbed.

Dilys Eaton *tells of a busy morning at Park Prewett.*

The Chaplains were busy on the wards and arranging services; as there was only one chapel to serve all denominations there always had to be some arrangements between them. Some nurses, Charge Nurses in particular, often brought their children in on Christmas morning and it was rather charming to see small children carefully carrying large platefuls of food to the patients. Our patients loved having children on the ward and it did bring a touch of the real world into what, with the best of intentions, could not fail to be an institutionalised life. They were frequently interrupted at this point by the Physician Superintendent leading a procession of the Management Committee, the Mayor and Mayoress and the odd doctor, doing a tour of the hospital.

Catherine Metcalfe's *father was busy there too.*

As my father became a leading male nurse at Park Prewett, he had to go up to the hospital on Christmas morning and carve the turkey in the various wards, then have a drink and move on to the next ward and carve the turkey in that ward - sometimes leading, perhaps, to rather too much alcohol!

Jo Kelly *knew what she was missing in the 1950s.*

Although I lived in Basingstoke, I spent a lot of my childhood in and out of Treloar Hospital in Alton. The build up to Christmas was great as we made miles, well yards, of paper chains that were then hung round the ward. We had tinsel wound round our bed frames, we made our cards for family and friends. Other children would talk of Christmas Day itself and how Father Christmas would arrive and give out presents, at least two for each child and sometimes three AND you could have two helpings of ice-cream. I never found out for myself because my Mother would arrive and take me home for Christmas. Of course it was lovely being home and being made much of but a part of me wished I could have stayed for just one Christmas Day, just to have seen it for myself. When I was taken back, the decorations would have disappeared and the ward sister's routine would have been re-established. No more double rations of ice-cream. But our house was always full at Christmas. Mum, Dad, Granddad, Great-uncle Charlie, then anyone Mum or Dad thought might be alone at Christmas; usually we had at least a dozen sitting down to Christmas dinner.

Joan Bull *remembers fewer round the table during the war years.*

We only managed one Christmas with the whole family, three boys and three girls (two boys in the Royal Navy and Royal Artillery, two girls in the ATS and Land Army).

Graham Kirby's *mother had to stretch her resources in the 1930s.*

As for Christmases, well, with only £2.10s a week coming in, and all the children, there wasn't a great lot going around, but I must say we were never hungry, it was always a nice roast dinner Christmas Day. And we had all the children to play with. I had two older sisters and by then a younger sister and a younger brother so there was five of us.

Ruby Philpott describes her family's Christmas dinner and their afternoon entertainment. As bakers, they had a very large oven.

We had our Christmas dinner about three in the afternoon, and the turkey was always cooked in the bakehouse oven. We used to cook a lot of our neighbours' turkeys in our bakehouse oven, because it was easier for them, and the turkeys cooked better.

My Mother always bought something for a surprise. One year she bought a small billiard table, another year she bought a cinematograph, which was marvellous. When she bought it they told her to turn it quickly but she was deaf and she didn't hear, and when we put it on nothing moved and she got so cross and said, 'Oh blow the thing!' and turned it quickly and of course everything moved, so that was all right. It must sound silly to you in these days of television. It was ever so exciting, we used to belong to a library of films in London, so you could keep changing them, otherwise you would have had the same thing, and we used to have what they called Pathé Gazette News on it. The same news that you had at the cinema, and although it was all stale because it was days old, you thought it was all right.

Arthur Attwood's family had a good time too in the 1920s and '30s.

For Christmas dinner some would have roast beef, but for many it would be chicken, cockerel or goose and, of course, turkey for the more fortunate.

 When it came to the traditional Christmas pudding, each of us hoped that the threepenny 'Joey' would be in our particular portion.

There was no Queen's fireside chat to listen to after the Christmas dinner. Parents would snatch forty winks after the washing up and then it was games time.

The sideboard would be loaded with apples, oranges, mixed nuts, dates, home-made coconut ice, ginger wine, chocolates, sweets, etc, which would be continually passed round during a game of whist, dominoes, snakes and ladders or snap. We would all join in the fun, without someone saying: 'I must switch the TV on at 5.'

BWM
1961.
364

There would always be two or three boxes of crackers for Christmas Day and Boxing Day and, like the bran-tubs, they contained a variety of really good novelties.

In addition to paper hats and jokes there would be such things as miniature tops which spun, leaping frogs, whistles and paper fireworks. One popular type of firework featured a farmer with a shotgun aiming at a rabbit.

As the spark crept across the paper towards the gun we youngsters would wait for the report.

Tea time

Mary Felgate *loved tea time — and washing up!*

Tea time was absolutely magic because then we had the Christmas tree in the middle of the tea table, all the family round the table, even Auntie Dorothy who went eventually to New Zealand when I was three or four. And the table was laid with Mother's very best tea service, beautiful white fluted cups and saucers and plates with a delicate green pattern round them. But also the other magical thing was that not only were the candles lit but on the table there were perhaps eight little square tin lanterns with glass at the sides, and those had the candles lit.

Where I was sitting I could see a chick on the Christmas tree, I suppose it was made of some kind of stiffened cardboard, it was a rounded chick, but its head was on a coiled spring and when anybody touched it the head bobbed up and down. And I did want that chick! And I can remember crying when Father cut it off and said it had got Auntie Dorothy's name on it – but what I had off the Christmas tree I'm afraid I don't remember.

Crackers, of course, were always wonderful things at Christmas tea time. They were always bought from Ody's in Winchester Street, they were always Tom Smith's crackers, and they went off with the most satisfying crack, and there were really very nice toys in them in those days, something worth keeping, little toys to put in the dolls' house or to play with. There would be tiny tops and whistles and all sorts of things.

One of the extra excitements was the Christmas crackers which had fireworks in them. This was a bit later. There was always a snail shell stuffed with something or other, with a little string showing, which Father lighted with a match. We waited and suddenly a long thick grey worm started to curve out of the shell, twisting as it emerged and with a simply terrible smell, which we loved. The worm eventually stopped emerging when it was about eight or ten inches long.

Another was a piece of paper with pictures on it, perhaps of two people with guns facing targets. Father put a lighted match head to the end of the guns and a tiny line of glowing red followed the line to the targets; when it reached them there was a sudden tiny sparking pop from the gunpowder and it was exciting to see whose man won.

Possibly from the time when I was eight, nine or even ten, Father taught me one of his favourite Christmas songs and he and I always used to sing it together, it became quite a tradition. Father was very good at washing up after Christmas tea. Mother had just about done enough every day during Christmas, so Father used to wash up the tea things particularly and I would wipe up, and he taught me this song to sing. Well, I'd got a nice little voice and he and I used to sing it together. I used to sing the tune and he, having a very lovely tenor voice, used to harmonise. Well, I'll try and sing it – I can't sing now, of course, like I used to, but at least I can put it on record with the words.

When I'm at school my father
Is working on the fa-a-arm
The harvest he must gather
And fold the earth from harm.
My brother's gone to sea,
My sister is from home.
She must at service be
Till merry Christmas co-o-o-ome.
Merry, merry, merry, merry Christmas bells
so sweetly sweetly chi-ime
Let your happy music on the breezes swell,
Oh Merry Christmas time.
Peace on earth,
Goodwill to men
And angels sing and sing again
While hearts and voices here below
Take up the glad refrai-ai-ai-ain
Merry, merry, merry merry Christmas bells
so sweetly sweetly chi-ime
Let your happy music on the breezes swell,
Oh Merry Christmas time.

When I was very young, Father always performed his conjuring tricks after tea when all had been cleared away, the Christmas tree had been moved back into the other room and the gas was lit. He produced packets with little pieces of paper inside, and pretended to take magic photographs without opening the packets. Then he did something to them, whether warming them by the fire, or putting them in water I cannot remember, but when they were opened afterwards there were real sepia photographs on the paper, mainly views, probably in Japan.

After that, we always played table games. Happy Families, Passing the Ring, Passing the Sixpence (at which Grandpa Langdon used to cause confusion and laughter as he usually produced another sixpence on his hand when someone was caught with the original one), Blow-football, Snakes and, Ladders, Ludo and many others. Word-making and I-Spy were favourites.

Mary gave these games to the Willis Museum: Solitaire and a version of SNAP with nursery-rhyme characters: Baa Baa Black Sheep, Jack & Jill, Little Bo-Peep, Humpty Dumpty, Little Jack Horner, the Old Woman who lived in a shoe, Old Mother Goose, Little Boy Blue and Old Mother Hubbard.

ACM 1968.212 ↓ ACM 1968.250 ↑

Ruby Philpott's *family in Potter's Lane enjoyed their day.*

We had our tea about five or so. We always had a Christmas tree but we didn't have that till after tea, so in the afternoon we had a lucky dip. We had a tub full of bran or something and had lucky dips. We had supper about ten-ish, cold turkey etc. We were always very late birds and then we didn't go to bed till about one or two, which was nice.

Owen Blissett *remembers a succession of family parties.*

I was born in George Street, Basingstoke, where I spent the first eight years of my life before coming to Kempshott in 1938. I don't know when 'Mickey Mouse' was 'born', but I do remember having a Mickey Mouse cardboard face mask from Father Christmas at Lanhams' Department Store in Winchester Street. As a result my Mother made a fancy dress for me, black stockings, red shorts, a black top, plus the mask, a 'perfect' Mickey Mouse, who distributed the presents at her party.

My mother had six sisters and one brother; four of the sisters lived in Basingstoke so there were something like three Christmas parties to attend over the Christmas period, plus one at my Granny's on Christmas Day.

Christmas party tea consisted of cold pork or tinned meat, pickles of all sorts, all home-made, I might say (no Sainsbury's or Tesco's in those days), sausage rolls, cheese and celery, finished off with jellies, trifles, Christmas cake and mince pies, with oranges and nuts for those not full up.

In 1937 or 1938 three of my cousins converted the cellar under their mother's and father's house into a cinema, decorated as for Christmas, with Christmas trees and fairy lights, and they purchased a ciné projector and hired films (silent, of course). So, after their mother's party, the whole families, something like 20 bodies altogether, crowded into the cellar for an evening's entertainment. Talk about Health and Safety!

After the success of the film show it was agreed that each family would contribute one penny (in old money) per week to a film fund towards the hire of films for the following year, and my father was elected treasurer.

Christmas parties all started at my Grandmother's on Christmas Day, followed by my Aunt Jinny's on Boxing Day, and hence to my other aunts and my mother, on convenient days afterwards.

In September 1939 the Second World War broke out, but we still held our Christmas parties, though we had to contend with the blackout and the lack of bus services.

I can well remember the Christmas party my mother and father held at that time - no buses, so there was a sleep-over, some of the men slept in arm chairs, the ladies slept five in a bed, three one way and two the opposite way, I slept on the ironing board between two arm chairs, and some of the older nephews walked back to Basingstoke from Kempshott. Our next door neighbour and his wife spent the evening with us. He was a GPO telephone engineer and was on 24 hour standby, so he installed a telephone in my mother's house via an extension cable through his front door letter box and thence through my mother's letter box. It was not until thirty years after this that my mother and father had a telephone of their own.

*For **Jessie Jack** at the Shrubbery, it had been a long day.*

After being on duty from half past seven in the morning till nine o'clock at night, we often walked home unless friends or relatives came for us in cars. And then on Boxing Day most of us had a half day. It was the fairest way to do it.

Boxing Day

A notice reproduced in A History of Basingstoke *by **Baigent & Millard** reports an unusual day for a local election as a result of the Municipal Corporations Act, 1835.*

Election for Town Councillors (under the new Act)

The election took place on Saturday, the 26th December, and the result of the polling was officially declared on the following Monday.

---

*Traditionally, Boxing Day was when various tradesmen came for their 'Christmas boxes', as **John Ferguson** explains.*

The postman, the dustman, the butcher, the baker (the candlestick maker, if you like) all got Christmas boxes. There were so many men. The coalman came and brought the coal in sacks on his shoulder and heaved it into the coal shed. His name was Mr Baughurst, and I'm sure he got a Christmas box.

***Brian Spicer** found that even a policeman might be offered a drink!*

In the time of the first Lord Camrose (from the end of the War to 1953) Lord Camrose used to ask the police to lay on extra patrols around Hackwood at holiday time. One Boxing Day P C Padwick came on his bike and Lord Camrose sent the butler over. 'Catch that kind P C who looks after us and ask him to come in for a drink.'

P C Padwick (later Superintendent Padwick) used to confess that he probably had more than one drink, as on the way home his foot became entangled between the cross bar and the pedals on his bike.

In **Within Living Memory** *Diana Stanley* *describes Hunt Breakfasts. Colonel John May was Mayor 6 times between 1883 and 1902.*

One of the special yearly events was Colonel John May's Hunt Breakfast on Boxing Day. The May family had lived in Basingstoke for some generations and Colonel John May in particular is remembered by the old people of the town for his many benefactions.

On Boxing Day he entertained members of the Hunt to a champagne meal in the Town Hall; at the same time, outside on trestle tables, beer and cheese were provided for anyone who was prepared to fight a way through the crowd. Farmers rode in from the country - some from ten or more miles away - stabling their horses at the Wheatsheaf or one of the other inns and then proceeding on foot, through the dense mass of people, to the Town Hall - by far the worst part of the journey. Barrels of beer and enormous quantities of cheese were consumed and no doubt a good time was had by all. When the time came for the ride home, before two fields had been crossed, there were numbers of empty saddles.

Susan Walker *used to enjoy the Vine Hunt in the mid to late 1950s.*

Always on Boxing Day, the hunt met in Basingstoke. This would be the Vine Hunt in those days. I think it has now been amalgamated to the Vine and Craven, but in those days it was just the Vine. They could meet, in the early days, in the yard at the Wheatsheaf, Winton Square, but later on it did move to the Market Place and meet there.

They would move off along London Street and then we would go up the Reading Road and out towards Chineham. It seemed to be mainly around Chineham and through Basing. The huntsman would be up in front, sounding the horn, and the hounds in front. And, as a rider or follower, you were never supposed to get in front of the huntsman. That was very frowned upon. My pony did not know these rules, I'm afraid, and I was not very strong. I've got a horrible feeling that at times we did get in front of him when we shouldn't have done.

Betty Blake used to watch it too.

It was customary for the Mayor to attend this gathering, which usually attracted quite a large crowd of onlookers. This was certainly a very colourful spectacle.

Deborah Woodland *puts a question to our readers.*

Does anyone else remember going to the War Memorial Park to see the boxing on Boxing Day about 1966? A ring had been set up just beyond the swings, on the edge of the open area used for the Carnival Tattoos. We watched it, all muffled up with hats and coats and scarves on. I remember the reds and blues of the decorations and I'm sure we saw this spectacle two years running – the ring was the same and we didn't stay for long because we'd seen it before! But I've spoken to a few people more or less the same age as myself and nobody else seems to remember it. I hope I haven't spent 40-odd years remembering that for it not to be true!

Betty Godden has this photo from 1946.

In the evening the St Michael's Guild held their Boxing Day party at Church Cottage. In later years the St Michael's Twenties Club continued the custom.

*Pantomimes often began on Boxing Day and **Arthur Attwood** reports a spectacular one at the Grand Theatre, the fore-runner of today's Haymarket.*

On May 16, 1925, the Grand was gutted by fire. Only the external walls and the girders in the roof remained and it looked as if Basingstoke had seen the last of its old Corn Exchange. But the building was restored, the columns supporting the roof were removed, the roof constructed in one span and the interior remodelled after the style of a theatre. It continued to be used, mainly as a cinema, with plays by amateur and professional companies staged occasionally.

After the Grand reopened, Mr Casey presented *Robinson Crusoe* as his annual pantomime and claimed it to be 'the most gorgeous pantomime ever produced in Basingstoke'.

Hannah Williams has always loved the BATS pantomime.

As a family we always booked our tickets for Boxing Day to go to the BATS (Basingstoke Amateur Theatrical Society) pantomime at the Haymarket Theatre. The whole town used to go.

They did all the traditional stuff of Dick Whittington, Aladdin, Cinderella etc but they did it in their own unique way. Kate Webb often played the Principal Boy. Martin Webb and Len Annakin used to play the dames - they were natural comedians and Len used to put in lots of jokes, local things. They involved children, usually associated with members of the company and there have been occasions in BATS when you've had three generations of one family - grandmother, son and then his son, all in the same production.

I've always preferred the home-grown pantomimes and look back on them with great nostalgia.

Christmas week

In **Jane Austen: A Life** *Claire Tomalin* mentions Christmas balls.

Eliza Chute was exactly the sort of young woman you would expect to become a friend of the Austen sisters ... She was gentle and sometimes uncertain of herself, very nervous, for example, about appearing at public balls that first Christmas in Hampshire, when her mother wrote to her, 'I am glad for your sake there are no Minuets at Basingstoke, I know the terror you have in dancing, not that you have any occasion for such fears.'

From **Ethel Lizzie Moody's** *diary, 1895. There was a large room for concerts and dances above the Powell shop.*

30 Monday
Went to a dance in H. Powell's Room. Was very jolly, had to come home at 11.30. Rosie Taylor went with us and came to sleep with us. Pale blue and velvet.

Betty Godden *enjoyed spending her Christmas money.*

In 1934 I was taken, after Christmas, to Lanham's in Winchester Street with my Christmas gift money. On arrival my mother was ushered by Mr Sealey, the Shop Walker, to a chair so that we could be served. The whole reason for the visit was for me to buy my Teddy Bear and I think he cost ten shillings. I still have my teddy bear, although for a number of years he was 'on loan' to my son.

New Year's Eve

*From **Ethel Lizzie Moody's** diary, 1895.*

> *31 Tuesday*
> *Slept till 9 o'clock. Rose T. and I had breakfast in bed. Rosie*
> *went home by the 10 train for a week's holiday. Went for a*
> *walk in the afternoon with Annie and Ada. All went to mid-*
> *night service.*

***Mary Felgate** had to work late.*

It's 1994 New Year's Eve, waiting for 1995. And my mind has gone
back to about 1933 or 34, when I was working in the bank in Reading,
and of course over the New Year was always our busy time, the same
as the June balance was always a busy time, at least for these three
weeks. So while everybody else was out enjoying themselves we were
working noses to the grindstone! I can remember one night I had to
come home from Reading on the last train about eleven o'clock.

> An old custom is still observed of the Clergy, Choir and other
> Parishioners ascending the Tower [of St Michael's church] on
> New Year's Eve, to sing the Old Hundredth Psalm at Midnight,
> before and after which the Old Year is rung out and the New Year
> rung in.
>
> ### *Baigent & Millard*

***Mary Felgate** tells of the bells, the choir - and the trains.*

One year, a most beautiful wonderful frosty night with full moonlight,
we went down to stand quite close to the tower of St Michael's to
listen to the choir singing up on top of the tower as the New Year came
in - it was the most magical night! At New Year when the church bells
rang all the trains in the station used to hoot their whistles - all
different notes. We used to wait for that.

New Year's Day

*A New Year Card sold in **Mary Felgate's** grandmother's shop.*

New Year gifts

These gifts to Henry VIII were mentioned in **A History of the Vyne in Hampshire.**

New Continental styles would have been evident in many of the gifts given at Court, particularly the New Year gifts bestowed by and upon the King, for example the pair of silver candlesticks given to Henry by Sandys at New Year 1532, or the gilt cup with cover presented by Lady Sandys to the sovereign at the same time.

Gifts from the Mayor mentioned in **The Mays of Basingstoke.**

On New Year's Day 1902 there floated bravely on the flagstaff of the Town Hall a handsome flag, emblazoned with the 'Borough Arms', the gift of the Mayor to the town, and which he formally presented to the Corporation at the monthly meeting in January. Since then the flag has always been flying when the Corporation have been sitting.

New Year Prospects

The significance of the New Year was vividly expressed by an article in **The Hants & Berks Gazette, January 1880.**

THE OLD AND THE NEW YEAR

The year 1879 has drawn to a close and its successor has been welcomed as a relief by many persons who, tired of the old year, are hopefully anticipating a brighter time to come. It is always thus at birthdays or new year days when individuals or communities are intent upon making a fresh start upon their career, after brief festivity to celebrate the accomplishment of one and the commencement of another. But this time there is now more than usual reason why people should be glad of the termination, and anticipate sanguinely improved prospects to come.

The article went on to describe exceptional meteorological conditions - prolonged winter frosts, a dull and forbidding spring, a summer that was never really warm and a wet autumn, leading to bad harvests and poor trade.

Only towards the close of the year did there begin to be a revival, rather noted by the barometer of trade returns than felt by individuals. These indications were welcomed for what they promised in regard to the new year rather than for what they implied in respect of the old. It is natural, then, that we may expect very soon after entering the new 'corridor of time' to feel the benefits of reviving trade, and a sort of faith in the doctrine of chances forbids us to expect another ungenial spring and summer. The deficiencies in the physical and commercial world which have marked the year 1879 have certainly not been made up by any great political or social achievement or good fortune. Home politics have spun out a humdrum sort of existence. The parliamentary crop was as deficient as the agricultural harvest, and political parties have continued to wrangle, to the wearying of many persons, over the old bone of contention, the foreign policy of the Government. Into the merits of that policy we shall not now enter. We may well anticipate better fortune in the coming time, and at least one satisfaction for the past can no longer be delayed - the submission of the ministerial policy and doings of a whole septennium to the judgment of the country. Altogether, there is reason to welcome the new year, which, we trust, will be a fortunate one to the country, and individually to each of our readers.

Does any of this sound familiar today?

In the New Year

Pantos at Park Prewett

*At Park Prewett Hospital, Pantomimes were put on after New Year's Day. **Susan Richmond** enjoyed them during World War 2 when she was secretary to the Director of the Emergency Medical Service.*

We used to have marvellous pantomimes and they were held at Rooksdown, which was the faciomaxillary, the skin-grafting unit under Professor Sir Harold Gillies. The two orthopaedic surgeons - they both had the same surname, Ellis, - were very gifted and they used to write the pantomime and all these doctors used to go into the pantomime. They were so funny because there was a great take-off of all the things going on in the hospital.

*When she became Hospital Librarian in 1954, **Dilys Eaton** discovered she had some unexpected duties.*

Once the New Year's Eve party was out of the way, THE PANTOMIME dominated our lives. This really was a community project, 'from each according to his ability'. The Works Department built the sets, the Art Therapist painted the cloths, the electricians did the lighting, the Sewing Room made brilliant costumes - and the Librarian did the make-up. In my first innocent Christmas as hospital librarian, the Entertainments Officer came into the library, carrying a large box which he deposited on my desk. 'The Librarian,' he said, 'has always done the pantomime make-up. May we count on you?'

The box, when opened, breathed the intoxicating smell of grease paint and, mercifully, also contained a book on stage make-up. I was hooked. I recruited a team of assistants and we worked right up to the last pantomime.

The pantomime cast was largely, though not exclusively, staff, with a few patients. One of the men played the giant for years. One of my duties, at his request, was to push him gently on stage when his cue came. A very large girl played the fairy. There was never any shortage of would-be thesps at the auditions and sometimes a quite unexpected talent was revealed. The Stores staff tended to come out strong as Brokers' Men and various comic characters. The bulk of the chorus was usually nurses, while staff children were the fairies and elves of the children's chorus. The Principal Girl was usually played by a pretty Student Nurse. The hospital band became the pit orchestra, conducted by the Entertainments Officer, wearing my husband's old tail coat, which he had donated to the prop box.

The Pantomime ran for a week and the traditional last night party took the form of a jolly good supper provided by the kitchen, which was attended by all; the cast still high on adrenalin, the rest of us exhausted.

Catherine Metcalfe remembers them in the late 1940s/50s and again in 1958-60.

From being a child I used to go and watch the pantomimes, and certain members of staff were always part of the cast. I remember someone called Harold Constadine, the father of a friend of mine, who was always one of the Brokers' Men or one of the baddies, and we got used to shouting and jeering at him when he came on the stage.

He's behind you!!

When I was about 16 I had two years when I was involved with the pantomimes. We practised from September to Christmas and they were a mixture of staff and the inmates of the hospital. I can remember one particularly good Demon King who was one of the patients, dressed in a green outfit with green face and green hair, and acted his part beautifully.

The second year, when we produced *Mother Goose*, the Mayor came to see the production and was so impressed with the work that the staff and patients had done that he asked that we should go to the Haymarket, and we had three nights in February at the Haymarket for the general public.

Jack and Jill and the Goose
Catherine is Jill (with a black wig) & Johnny Baldwin is the Dame.

Going to the Haymarket was a good move, but **Dilys Eaton** *found conditions rather cramped there.*

I had to paint the ducklings' faces yellow and white. It was back-breaking work, crouching to paint tiny faces of children about three feet high, as there was so little room behind the scenes at the Haymarket.

91

Owen Blissett *knew some 'behind-the-scenes' gossip.*

In *Mother Goose* the three Brokers' Men got in the audience, and got so carried away playing the fool that they forgot their characters' names and called each other by their real names.

The Engineers built the Goose, which was played by a boy who was a cadet nurse. They put a pump inside so that water squirted out of the Goose's eyes.

Any costumes that showed white were washed, dried and ironed every day of the run.

Catherine Metcalfe *liked the orchestra.*

The hospital had an orchestra, of course, and the orchestra accompanied the pantomime and the songs. Most of the orchestra were staff but there were one or two of the patients who played in the orchestra as well. The orchestra was very important because they played for dances, there were Christmas dances for patients, there were New Year's parties and dances for the staff, so they were really an integral part of the social life of the hospital.

Then there were parties and dances. **Dilys Eaton** *was particularly impressed by the Fancy Dress.*

The Pantomime was followed in short order by the Patients' Fancy Dress Dance - very short order indeed for the Sewing room, still catching its breath. Patients and ward staff went into huddles and came up often with imaginative offerings: an elderly man dressed as a gamekeeper, complete with shot gun (at the time of the Lady Chatterley scandal) and a very handsome woman in black velvet breeches and coat, with real silk stockings, as Dandini. Much as they enjoyed the pantomime, especially watching the staff make fools of themselves, the patients' favourite part of the Christmas entertainments was this Fancy Dress Dance, providing discussions of the costumes for several days before and after and much criticism of the judges' decision.

The Christmas gaieties concluded with another hospital stalwart, the Staff Annual Ball. This was a much more formal affair, with men in dinner jackets and the women in long dresses—black was advisable, less recognisable from year to year. A sort of unwritten three line whip ensured a full turnout of doctors, senior staff, committee members and, of course, the Mayor and Mayoress, sitting on the red leather chairs in front of the stage and below the band, a position that precluded conversation. But everyone was there, the hall was always full and the floor always crowded. Unsophisticated we may have been; archaic we may have been, as a rather patronising guest once called us, but patients and staff enjoyed a Park Prewett Christmas and New Year.

93

Hospital pantos continued . . .

The Basingstoke District Hospital, now the North Hampshire & Basingstoke Hospital Trust, has continued the tradition of putting the annual pantomime on at the Haymarket Theatre.

John Ramage *explains why the timing changed.*

The Hospital panto used to be put on before Christmas but it was just too difficult to organise both the theatre and all the people. It's actually better having it in the first week or two of January, and the audience is better then because there's not much to do in the first two weeks of January apart from go to the theatre.

Julie Jones *has already told us why the cast includes consultants, but could there be a problem?*

There is a danger, with having consultants taking part in the panto, that they might have to rush off to some emergency operation in the middle of a performance. My biggest nightmare is a major incident, because the majority of the cast would be called to it. And probably the majority of the audience!

When you're on the stage, you could be the domestic, standing next to a consultant, but you're all doing the same job. Everybody gets on really well because they've all got the same goal and you meet people you would never have met before. It's a really good morale-booster for people who have busy jobs and perhaps are tired or sad and they go up there and they have a laugh.

__John__ agrees that panto is good for the cast.

There have been a number of pantomime relationships, when people have met each other doing pantomime, got married and had children.

And __Julie__ says it is good for others too.

It's all done for charity, like the Medical Fund looking for a piece of equipment, Hospital Radio or the Physio Gym where we rehearse, and also community charities like Home Start.

Twelfth Night

From a review by **Susan Good** *in the Basingstoke Archaeological &
Historical Society's* **Newsletter 151**, *February 2001.*

I wonder how many of you who attended **A Celebration through
Paintings over several centuries of the Visit of the Three Kings
to Christ's Nativity** in Church Cottage on January 6th discovered,
as you took down your Christmas cards on Twelfth Night (the
feast of the Epiphany) that you had been sent reproductions of
some of the masterpieces featured in the illustrated lecture given
by Miss Jane Baker, former Keeper of Fine Art at The Royal
Albert Memorial Museum, Exeter. The scene was set for this
interesting and informative talk by Mr Paul Connolly's
atmospheric reading of T S Eliot's *Journey of the Magi*, before
Miss Baker reminded the audience that 12th to 17th century art
had been kept alive both by the churches, who commissioned
paintings and frescoes, and later by the patronage of wealthy
families, such as the Medici. As Miss Baker commented, 'When
the ordinary things of life have been dealt with, Art is the icing on
the cake'. She also described the great processions held in
Florence to celebrate Epiphany, which could be seen in many of
the Italian paintings. Miss Baker's enthusiastic and clear
interpretation of her slides enabled the audience to see the way
that representation of the Three Kings had evolved, whilst still
retaining the essential religious message.

Just as Christmas seemed to start early, sometimes New Year goes on well into January. I'm sure the **Basingstoke Hockey Club** intended this Annual Dance as a New Year event, so we conclude with a real treasure, a dance card with the names of partners pencilled in. At first we thought this was a very energetic young lady, but it looks as if some of the names—very faint—might be Mrs or Miss X. And the initials on the front are JEW—could this be Mr J E Whittingham, one of the MCs or Stewards? We can tell you that T O Barlow was a pharmaceutical chemist in Market Square in 1902 and Frank Moody was the brother of Ethel Lizzie Moody whose diary is quoted throughout this book. Mr John M Gammon was a Borough Councillor and in 1903 had an outfitter's shop in Winchester Street—we even have a collar stud from his shop.

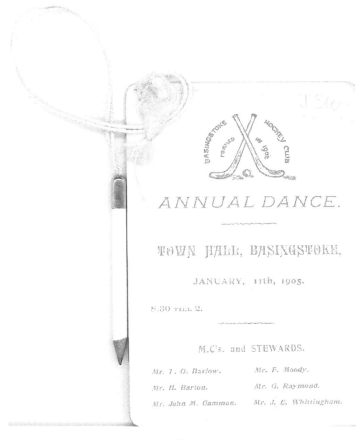

ANNUAL DANCE.

TOWN HALL, BASINGSTOKE,

JANUARY, 11th, 1905.

8.30 TILL 2.

M.C's. and STEWARDS.

Mr. T. O. Barlow.   Mr. F. Moody.

Mr. H. Barton.   Mr. G. Raymond.

Mr. John M. Gammon.   Mr. J. E. Whittingham.

97

PROGRAMME.

	Dances.	Engagements.
1. POLKA.	Whistling Rufus.	
2. WALTZ.	Ivy.	
3. LANCERS.	Country Girl.	
4. WALTZ CHAIN	Selected.	
5. BARN DANCE	Canadian.	
6. WALTZ.	Reverie.	
7. LANCERS.	Gondoliers.	
8. WALTZ.	Choristers.	
9. POLKA.	Hiawatha.	
10. LANCERS.	Haddon Hall.	

Interval.

11. WALTZ.	Donan Wetten.	
12. BARN DANCE	Floradora.	
13. POLKA.	Mosquito Parade.	
14. LANCERS.	Chinese Honeymoon.	
15. WALTZ.	Tendresse.	
16. LANCERS.	Orchid.	
17. WALTZ CHAIN	Selected.	
18. WALTZ.	Floradora.	
19. LANCERS.	Artist's Model.	
20. { WALTZ & GALLOP.	Sonnenschein & John Peel.	

We hope you have enjoyed these reminiscences of Christmas and the New Year in Basingstoke.

Interviews

The recorded interviews from which the extracts in this book were taken are held in the Wessex Film & Sound Archive, (Hampshire Record Office, Winchester) and their accession numbers are given below in the series M, BAHS or BTH, as well as page references. Some extracts were not recorded (V = verbal; W = written). The cassettes, CDs or transcriptions of the full interviews can be accessed at WFSA, the Willis Museum Resources Centre or the Basingstoke Archaeological & Historical Society.

Nita Abbott, p 48 *BAHS 149 BTH 3*; **Hilda Applin**, pp 11-12 *M 6, BAHS 11*; **Bob Applin**, p 50 *BTH 1*; **John Ashlin**, pp 54, 65 *M 49/50*; **Robin Attwood**, p 67, *V;* **Peggy Barker**, p 49 *BAHS 98;* **Betty Blake**, pp 21-22, 81 *BAHS 126, 138, W*; **Owen Blissett**, pp 12, 41, 77-78, 92 *BAHS 132, W*; **Robert Brown**, pp 27, 68 *M 3, BTH 29*; **Joan Bull**, pp 38, 49, 67, 71 *BAHS 66, 109*; **Brian Butler**, pp 36, 61 *BAHS 47, W*; **Geoffrey Butler**, p 64, *W*; **Jean Chivers**, pp 46-47 *BAHS 31*; **Irene Compton**, p 69 *BTH 21*; **Paul & Ann Connolly**, p 44 *BAHS 145, BTH 22*; **Dilys Eaton**, pp 13-14, 70, 89-91, 93, *W;* **Margaret Evans**, p 41 *BAHS 143*; **Mary Felgate**, pp 17, 36, 53-54, 59-60, 63, 74-76, 85 *M 19, 34, 47, BAHS 146-148*; **John Ferguson**, pp 29, 62, 64, 79 *BTH 30*; **Mary Fraser**, p 65 *BAHS 139*; **Harold Gates**, p 47 *BAHS 39/40*; **Betty Godden**, pp 22, 28, 34, 38, 40, 58, 65, 82, 84 *BAHS 60, BTH 36, W*; **Eric Godden**, pp 38 *BAHS 60, BTH 36, W*; **Barbara Green**, p 39 *BAHS 61*; **Jessie Jack**, pp 39, 69, 78 *M 18*; **Julie Jones**, pp 6-7, 94, 95 *BTH 34*; **Jo Kelly**, pp 26, 36, 43, 62, 71 *BTH 7, BAHS 20;* **Graham Kirby**, pp 22, 64, 71 *BTH 39;* **Catherine Metcalfe,** pp 43, 48-49, 71, 90-91, 92 *BTH 28*; **Hazel Montague-Ebbs**, p 70 *BTH 19*; **Ian Murray** p 34 *BTH 25*; **Sylvia North**, p 70 *BTH 31*; **Beryl Northcott**, p 42 *M 25*; **Neil Ogden**, p 58 *BTH 40*; **Audrey Peryer**, p 22 *BTH 20*; **Ruby Philpott**, pp 55, 62, 72, 77 *M 13*; **John Ramage**, pp 6-7, 94, 95 *BTH 34*; **Susan Richmond**, p 89 *M 29, 32*; **Brian Spicer**, pp 45, 79, *V, BAHS 29, 32-34*; **Michael Tarrant**, p 36 *BTH 18*; **Terry Tarrant**, pp 9, 15, 19 *BTH 33. V*; **Susan Walker**, pp 80-81 *BAHS 55*; **Hannah Williams**, pp 37, 44-45, 83 *BTH 23*; **Deborah Woodland**, pp 23, 34, 37, 38, 41, 51, 52, 58, 62 65, 82 *BTH 35*; **Pat Wright**, p 37 *BAHS 95.*

BASINGSTOKE ARCHAEOLOGICAL & HISTORICAL SOCIETY

(Registered Charity No.1000263)   www.bahsoc.org.uk

Secretary Ginny Pringle Tel: 01420 550028 secretary@bahsoc.org.uk

AIMS

■ To investigate the history and prehistory of the Borough of Basingstoke and Deane, and to stimulate interest in archaeological and historical studies generally

■ Lectures on the second Thursday of the month, September to May, 7.30 pm at Church Cottage, Church Square, Basingstoke. Visitors welcome, £2.

■ Visits to places of archaeological and historical interest

■ Fieldwork, training excavations and finds processing.

■ The Basingstoke Talking History project: to record, transcribe, research and, where appropriate, publish memories of Basingstoke's past. We welcome help in recording and transcribing interviews and in carrying out associated research, publication and displays.

■ Quarterly Newsletter and other publications.

Beneath Basingstoke the DVD
The Making of Basingstoke Eric Stokes
Taking the Pulse of Basingstoke ed Barbara Applin
Voices of Basingstoke 1400-1400 Anne Hawker
Going Down Church Street to the Felgate Bookshop
Mary Felgate and Barbara Applin
The Story of Basingstoke Anne Hawker
Roundabout Basingstoke Barbara Applin
Happy Christmas, Basingstoke! ed Barbara Applin